CHRONIC HOPE

Families and Addiction

Author

KEVIN PETERSEN, LMFT

Table of Contents

Author's Note

If you've ever asked the question, "What do we do with our family member whose drug use and drinking is out of control?" you are not alone. I started writing this book in 2017 with the intention of offering my answer to that question—one I get almost every day in my private therapy practice. I wanted to share my experience of being from an addicted family and how they helped me get sober.

I opened my practice in Denver, Colorado in 2014. From the first day forward, my clients were mainly parents who would call me and ask if they could bring their kid in to see me (the "kids" were all ages, from 16, 26, 36 on up) so I could help with their substance abuse issues. My response has always been the same: I would rather meet with the entire family to talk about how to address the substance abuse *and* the family system, not just the person using.

You have a much greater chance for success if the whole family, not just the addict, is engaged in recovery.

I knew my plan had to be quick and to the point so we could triage the immediate problem. Then, only once we put the initial fire out, would we spend more time addressing the bigger issues. My wife Amy convinced me that my message needed to be heard by more than one family at a time in my office. My friend, Scott Benton, offered to show me how to write a book. I am eternally grateful to both of them for getting me started and for not letting me quit.

It has been my experience that when a family comes into my office, they are looking for immediate impact and direction, not a philosophical or intellectual discussion. If you call the fire department because your house is engulfed in flames and they ask you how you feel about it instead of turning on their hoses, you would feel quite frustrated.

My approach is to turn on the hose first.

I created a plan that puts out the fire and *then* (and only then) says, "Let's talk about what we can do to make sure this does not happen again. We need to talk about the whole family."

When I was a kid growing up in Palo Alto, my dad constantly dragged me to the Stanford School of Business for seminars on entrepreneurship. These programs were given by visionaries who went on to become the legends of Silicon Valley. I didn't care who they were, I *hated* it. Nevertheless, I absorbed their message: the old way of doing business—the militaristic top-down way IBM and Xerox had done things for decades—was not the way forward. Instead of issuing orders and keeping track of every decision, the position of these innovators was more like, "We are going to empower people to solve their *own* problems."

They believed it was their job to be a cheerleader, to unleash the talented creators they had hired: "I'm here to help you, to empower you. I can't do it for you."

The same principle applies to what I teach the families of addicted individuals today: It's not about you standing watch over your loved one. It's about setting boundaries, setting expectations, and then saying, "If you need help, I'm here. In the meantime, I'm going to work on myself. We need to change this entire system."

My clients hire me to be a family consultant. Just as a company often hires a consultant to fix its business when things are not going well, families hire me to change the system when their family unit isn't functioning well. When you bring in a consultant, the first thing everyone at the company agrees on is that the business is failing. Therefore, *we have to change the way we do business.* Firing the receptionist is not going to do it; everything has to change. Also, when your consultant is telling you that you will have to change the way the family does business or you'll go broke, please listen. The definition of insanity is to do the same thing over and over and expect a different result. Ignoring what I tell you means you're willing to let it happen again.

I find this metaphor connects very well with families who are suffering because of addiction. It's not therapy-speak, it's just the truth.

I hope you find this book helpful in your time of crisis. I know this plan is not for everyone but it worked for me in 1991 and continues to work for my clients today.

Kevin Petersen, MA, LMFT, Founder of the Chronic Hope Institute

www.chronichope.us

Twitter: @TheChronicHope

Facebook: @ChronicHopeInstitute

Instagram: @TheChronicHopeInstitute

LinkedIn: www.linkedin.com/showcase/the-chronic-hope-institute/

chapter one

GROWING UP IN A HOUSE OF ADDICTION

Chapter 1

Growing Up in a House of Addiction

When I was growing up, my household had a lot of secrets. My mom was addicted to prescription drugs and my dad was extremely codependent with her. My sister and I didn't understand that this environment wasn't normal.

Mom had been a teacher and piano player. She had once won a dance contest doing The Twist in San Francisco. After growing up in McCloud, California, Mom graduated from Chico State University, which had a reputation as a party school. From what I have been told, my mother was very outgoing and had a vibrant personality before she gave birth to my sister and me. I'm unsure when exactly she started to use prescription drugs to manage her depression, anxiety, and pain issues. All I know is that I didn't grow up with the outgoing, vibrant woman many described her to be. Sometimes she'd start a health kick or begin meeting with a therapist and change into a fun woman I loved to be with. But these moments were brief and unpredictable.

My parents met in a bar in Mountain View, California in 1962. They married and moved to Palo Alto, California in 1969. Working in the profitable envelope and flat packaging industry, my father had a generous income, making it easy for my mom to never work and for my sister and me to have a comfortable, privileged lifestyle with a large home, golden retrievers, and lavish vacations.

Dad grew up in San Jose, California. His mom was an alcoholic and his dad was a salesman for Nabisco. As the oldest of three children, it was impressed upon him that he was responsible for his younger brother and sister. While my dad had many expectations placed upon him at an early age, I know he felt he never lived up to them. Just as my dad felt his role growing up was to take care of his siblings, he later felt his role as I grew up was to make money to afford our Palo Alto lifestyle and take care of my mom and all of her issues.

Each day, I would come home from high school to find my mom in her room with the lights off and the shades drawn, complaining of migraines. Whether she had real migraines or not I'll never know, but she did have several prescriptions in the medicine cabinet. When I was 14 years old, I couldn't pronounce the names on the bottles or determine what the drugs were used for, but it was evident these prescriptions put her in a daily stupor.

Perception vs. Reality

From the outside, out family looked like we had it all: money, cars, happy kids, and vacations. But it was a facade. We had a monster living in our home and no one knew about it. My mom would wear her pajamas and stay in bed all day. She would join us on outings to sports games or family events only occasionally. When she did join us, we were always hours late. To explain our tardiness, we always came up with an excuse. But we didn't only come up with excuses for why we were so late. As the responsible, dutiful son and daughter, we were caretakers. We came up with excuses for why my mom didn't join us out, excuses for why my parents couldn't answer the phone even though they were home, excuses for why it was me accompanying my dad to his college alumni events instead of my mom.

Continuing our caretaker roles, we often organized dinner for the family and handled common parental responsibilities. We wondered what my mom did all day. Why was she unable to take on some of the common responsibilities of a parent? I know now that one common trait of an addict is lack of awareness, meaning things don't register to them unless something directly affects the addict's own needs. At the time, I didn't understand why my mom demonstrated this lack of awareness toward her children. She often failed to demonstrate the qualities of a traditional parent, including reprimanding us. For example, when I received a speed contest and racing ticket as a teen and had my license suspended for 30 days, the next day my mom told me to drive to the pharmacy to pick up her prescriptions. Demonstrating an addict's lack of awareness, she didn't care that my license was suspended. She just needed her medications.

I could have gone to jail if I had been stopped. But to my mom, her drugs mattered more.

Traumatized, Anxious, Unsafe

One morning during the recent Covid-19 pandemic, I woke up and felt traumatized, anxious, and unsafe. This is *exactly* what it was like growing up in my household as a child. The emotions were the same.

A house of addiction is one in which the parents are at war. The addict often rules the roost, directly and indirectly. The addict will say things like, "You're all lucky I'm such a great provider. It's my way or the highway. If you don't like it, leave. How dare you question me? I can't believe you're related to me. Don't you dare talk about this to others." There's a big element of secrecy in houses of addiction. The irony is the same thing may be going on next door. Addiction is everywhere.

Then, there's generally someone trying to keep the peace when addiction is present in the household. The other parent, who is dealing with his or her own trauma or own anxiety, may say things like, "Your dad really does love you but he doesn't know how to show it. He's under a lot of stress at work and we really are lucky to have what we do. There are a lot of people who are less fortunate."

This is the denial process, the cover story: someone in the household is projecting the image of everything being okay. Unfortunately, it's living a lie and is incredibly disruptive to a child's emotional development.

This is what I heard a lot growing up: that I was lucky to grow up in Palo Alto and that I should shut up and keep the family's problems to myself. Infidelity and physical abuse are also often part of the equation in houses of addiction, so we have to talk about these things, too. The foundation of what's going on in the house will be mirrored by the children. Clients of mine who live in a house of addiction often say, "My kid hasn't seen anything. They don't know what's going on." I always reply, "They know *exactly* what's going on."

Five Common Coping Mechanisms

Children growing up in a house of addiction have five common reactions. It's possible to adopt multiple roles. I was both a caretaker and a flight risk.

- **The fighter:** This is the child who says, "Screw this, I'm going to step in. This is wrong and I'm going to take care of this." This is the kid who will be fighting at school, fighting at work. The fighter is a very angry, belligerent child, often the oldest. This response, of course, is all based in fear.

- **The flight risk:** This child runs, as in, "I'm out of here." This is the child who is always at a friend's house or staying over at the girlfriend's or boyfriend's place. They attach to other families to find the love and connection that they are not finding at home, which puts them at risk for predators and abuse. This kid leaves the house in the morning and doesn't return until very late. He has a job or participates in a lot of extra-curricular activities like sports teams to avoid being home as much as possible. I did this.

- **The freeze response:** This child tries not to see what is going on: "That's no big deal, this isn't happening. Everything is fine here." This kid is hiding out in their room, immediately disappearing when things get tense. They get sick a lot. They're terrified because they just don't know what to do. They feel overpowered by what's happening. This response is common among littler kids who cannot fight or leave. Also called The Ostrich, they stick their head in the sand and pretend it's not happening.

- **The clown:** This kid is the jester of the family. He is cute and funny in order to break the constant tension in the household and make everything okay. This child is trying to distract people with comedy or charm.

- **The caretaker:** This child generally ends up becoming a nurse, a teacher, or a therapist later in life (as I did). This is the one who hovers over everyone to protect them. It's the sibling who goes and gets dad from the bar or turns on the TV or the music to distract the younger kids when fighting or using occurs: "We're going to have a dance party!" It's a very common role.

A child growing up in this situation is looking for something — anything — to make themselves feel better. Children from these environments may turn to drugs, alcohol, being perfect at school, or getting too close to a boyfriend or girlfriend too quickly. A child raised in a house of addition may cling to a boyfriend/girlfriend relationship because the child likes that other more stable family.

I did drugs and alcohol at a young age. I also disappeared into school, into work, and into sports. I wanted to get my own money as soon as possible so I wouldn't have to be reliant on my parents or ask them for anything, tearing apart a sense of connection in the family. The question for me was always, "How do I make myself feel better? How do I make myself numb?" Today, children whose parents are addicts may turn to porn, gambling, shopping, or high-pressure academics. My high school alma mater, Palo Alto High School, has a very high suicide rate. Students there too often feel that they're not perfect, they're failures. It's a serious problem.

Today, I teach my clients that happy families come from happy individuals, and happy individuals work on their own stuff. The key thing to realize is you are not alone. You are not the only one dealing with this.

Growing Up in a House of Addiction

It wasn't until years later that I realized I had grown up in a house of addiction. Since I was 12 years old, how I lived—with my mom's reclusive behavior, her unusual amount of prescriptions, dad's codependency, and my caretaking responsibilities—was all I had ever known. My sister and I were the caretakers who cleaned up the messes and kept the secrets. Never did I question the caretaker-addict relationship because I simply thought how my family lived was normal.

But it wasn't. And while I spent many years of my childhood as the caretaker, I soon became an addict myself. Starting at 13 years old, I briefly drank and smoked marijuana with older boys while on camping trips with the Boy Scouts of America. Since sports and schoolwork kept me busy, I didn't lose control with alcohol or drugs until I enrolled at the University of Southern California in August 1982.

With a wealth of drugs and alcohol around me, I proceeded to drink and use drugs constantly, fail my classes, and mentally distance myself from my family. Meanwhile, in Palo Alto, my parents continued their facade but my mom didn't have me as one of her caretakers anymore. My dad threatened to leave my mom; my sister was frustrated that I wasn't there with them. She would call me and insist I come home for summer vacation but I dreaded it.

During my first year at USC, I kept the details about my self-destructive behavior from my family. Then in the summer 1983, my father and I were on a whitewater rafting trip and met John and Cristina Noble, a couple who owned a farm outside of Granada, Spain. They invited me to live with them and work on their farm. After making the quick decision that college was not for me, I purchased a plane ticket and promised my parents I'd return to USC after six months in Spain.

John and Cristina showed me unmatched kindness, generosity and hospitality, and I enjoyed working on their farm, exploring Spanish cities, and forgetting college. Reinventing oneself in the context of a new family is classic flight risk behavior and I was no exception to the rule. Unfortunately, I returned John and Cristina's benevolence with recklessness. After several drinks one evening, I drove their car off an eight-foot embankment and totaled it. Crashing the car and reflecting on John and Cristina's kindness, I went into a shame spiral filled with uncontrolled drinking.

After six months in Spain, my parents reminded me that I had agreed to return to USC. When I came home in December of 1983, frustration set in. I had enjoyed my time in Spain so much. The work had been simple and I had had the freedom to do whatever I wanted. In early 1984, John and Cristina had sent a postcard to me while on a safari. Jealous of their adventure, I turned to my mom and said, "See what I gave up to come home?"

She merely shrugged and said, "You could have stayed there. There's nothing we could have done about it."

Determined to defy my parents for the rest of my life, I vowed to never listen to them again. Returning to USC in the fall of 1984, I continued to struggle with drugs and alcohol over the next four years. Before long, I couldn't even register for classes due to academic probation, overdue tuition bills, and unresolved misconduct issues with the Dean of Student Life. By 1988, I had spent six years partying, using drugs, drinking incessantly, and wondering when I would graduate. After reviewing the paperwork to determine where I stood academically, I received a hand-written note from my academic advisor. The note explained I was not enrolled at all yet owed $10,000 and was still on both academic and behavioral probation.

Denial and Reckoning

As I mentioned, one feature of an addict is lack of awareness or denial. So, it's no surprise that after reading the letter from USC, I thought to myself, *I'm graduating in May!*

The graduation festivities began. I rented my cap and gown and mailed invitations to family and friends, letting them know about my graduation on May 9, 1988. I was drunk all week leading up to the graduation ceremonies. After attending the student-wide ceremony and the smaller ceremony for the Economics Department, I proudly received my empty diploma holder and partied with my friends and family. While I expected to be cornered, called a fraud, and publicly humiliated at any moment, it never happened.

When I moved back to Palo Alto, I spent two years bartending and selling marijuana. I knew a steady, well-paying job wouldn't be possible until I truly graduated college and had a degree to prove it. In August of 1990, my family hosted a four-day family reunion in Templeton, California. I was drunk the entire time and spent most of it with my cousin Nels, wasted on the front porch of the family home. My dad offered to drive me home to Palo Alto. Within the first five minutes of our four-hour drive, he turned to me.

"Kevin, you are my only son, and I love you, but I can't tolerate your drinking anymore," he said. "I know you didn't actually graduate from USC two years ago, and since then, you sold the BMW I gave you and are bartending and wasting your life. Your mother, your sister, and I are not dealing with you anymore until something changes."

This wasn't the first time my parents had tried the tough love act. They always caved eventually, so I argued with my dad during the ride home, telling him he didn't love me or trust me, and that my bad decisions were his fault. Despite my insults, he told me I wasn't welcome at the house. He said if I did drop by unannounced, he'd call the police.

After my dad dropped me off at my apartment, I started my usual routine of drinking and using drugs, knowing that once my dad simmered down, I could talk my way out of the tough love act.

I was wrong.

Dr. Julian Grodsky

My dad didn't budge, and after six weeks of exile from the family, I did what all "tough guy" addicts do: I called my mom. After crying about dad's unfairness and complaining how hard my life was, my mom didn't offer a sympathetic ear. Instead, she told me to start seeing a therapist with my dad.

This was a common tactic in the family: work out your issue with a doctor or therapist, then come back to the family and don't talk about it anymore. My parents had been sending me to therapists since I was 14 years old, so I thought I would bullshit another therapist as I had for over a decade, get my privileges back, and return to my partying. Starting in January 1991, I met with my dad and his therapist, Dr. Julian Grodsky, every Thursday morning. During these meetings, I began to tell the truth. I admitted to faking my graduation at USC; I owned up to the drinking and the drugs.

At the same time, my dad started to tell the truth about his life as well. Dad elaborated on his experiences growing up: how his mother was an alcoholic, how his brother and his sister struggled with alcohol, how his father had debilitating Parkinson's disease. He described the expectations placed upon him as a kid and said the unhealthy dynamic still existed with his mother, brother, and sister. Dad admitted that he felt like a fraud in Palo Alto, as he was a working-class kid from San Jose who didn't belong with affluent, sophisticated executives. But he stuck it out because he wanted his kids to have access to schools and a life that he didn't experience.

One morning in late April of 1991, my parents went out of town for my mom's birthday. I went to therapy alone. I told Dr. Grodsky we could pick up where we left off from the previous week, but Dr. Grodsky said he had something he wanted to talk about with me.

"I think you are an alcoholic and a drug addict, and you need help," he said.

This was certainly not the first time I had been told I had a problem. Everyone from friends to girlfriends to employers to health professionals had all confronted me about my drinking and drug use for years. But I found I couldn't disagree with Dr. Grodsky. For the previous four months, I had poured out my secrets to him and to my dad.

I asked what I should do. Dr. Grodsky recommended a friend of his named Dr. Barry Rosen, a specialist in alcoholism and addiction.

Admitting to my addiction felt like removing the weight of the world from my shoulders. During the following week's therapy session, I admitted to my dad that I was an alcoholic, and I could see the relief in his eyes. He said something like, "That explains everything! You are just too damn smart to keep screwing up so much." After drinking at a wedding that weekend, I began my journey to sobriety on Sunday, May 5, 1991.

My Comprehensive Addiction Perspective

I've been in all the roles within the caretaker-addict relationship: I was a caretaker for my mom; I was an addict, and then the addict-turned-sober. Today, I am a licensed mental health professional. Maybe you've been or are in one of these roles, too. My personal experience, seeing how an addiction ran in my family, being an addict myself, going into recovery, and engaging in the challenge of healing an entire family, drives what I do today.

Dr. Grodsky and my dad helped me develop a plan to sobriety, which included actually securing a degree from USC. Of course, re-enrolling into the school I had wasted six years partying in wasn't going to be easy. I knew it would take discipline, determination, and humility, starting with a visit with the secretary of the president at USC. My hope was that securing a job at USC would allow me to attend school part-time tuition-free. I contacted my friend, Liz King, who was the president's secretary. After explaining my plan to seek a job and enroll at USC, Liz scheduled an appointment for me to speak with her at 8 am on Monday,

June 3, 1991. I admitted to her that I had never actually graduated. She simply smiled.

"Kevin, I am the Secretary to the President of USC, I am well aware of the fact that you didn't graduate. There are quite a few people you will need to meet before you can enroll," Liz said. "But first, I want you to run over to the Athletic Department and meet with a friend of mine named Ron Orr."

I thought Liz had secured a job for me at the USC Athletic Department. After being escorted to a nearby office, I met Ron: a guy who looked just like me. He was a former swimmer and fraternity guy—and an alcoholic.

"My name is Ron," he said, shaking my hand. "I am an alcoholic, and I would like to take you to a meeting tonight, if you're available."

That Monday evening began my journey into 12-Step Programs for Addiction Recovery. While I had managed to stay sober from May 5 to June 3 on pure will-power, personal will-power isn't sustainable without the power of a support system. I had planned to live in my former fraternity house for the summer as it was inexpensive and close to campus.

While the other guys living there were either working or attending summer school classes, they also partied.

Fortunately, I soon secured a job counseling parents and students on tuition and expenses payment at the Office of Financial Services, working for Peter Tom. Kind, patient, and unafraid to hold me accountable, Peter supported me on my road to sobriety. In January 1992, I began my second round as a student at USC. I was entirely unprepared for the workload from my classes, plus my full-time job and daily 12-Step meetings. The next two and a half years had its ups and downs. Often, I felt overwhelmed with school courses. I was reprimanded at work for falling behind at times. Yet the people who came into my life over those two and a half years—Dr. Grodsky, Liz, Ron and Peter—were my personal angels. They helped guide me to sobriety.

In August 1994, I graduated from USC with a Bachelor of Arts degree in Social Sciences. A year later, I moved to Colorado. My sister had moved to Boulder, Colorado in 1993, and I knew after visiting her a few times that it was where I wanted to be.

Hitting a Wall and Finding a Reset

The following few years were a whirlwind. I quickly found my 12-Step community in both Denver and Boulder. I lived with my cousin, Joe, and worked in a series of successful sales roles at various companies.

But when I got married in 2002 and divorced in 2005, I hit a wall in my journey of sobriety. My ex-wife was unfaithful to me. And while I continued to step-parent her two children after the divorce, my ex-wife believed that I was at fault for all the things she was struggling with and in January of 2007 told me that I could no longer spend time with them unless I was willing to pay her more money every month. I spoke with a lawyer about fighting for custody and she told me that since my ex had not allowed me to adopt them, I had no rights. I never saw the children again and sank into depression that kept me in an auto-pilot motion for the next few months.

At 43 years old and 16 years sober, I was extremely unhappy. I was no longer able to see the step-children I loved and was burned out from the grueling sales roles I held that brought in a high salary with minimal personal fulfillment.

The question became, should I go back to graduate school or continue in my cushy role in sales?

I began reevaluating what *did* make me happy: helping others and seeing people piece their lives together, as addicts across the nation do in 12-Step Programs. For 16 years, my 12-Step meetings had kept me mentally afloat. So, I quit my sales job and applied to a graduate program focused on counseling at Regis University. While attending an open house event, I cornered the Dean of Students, John Armand, and asked him if I was wasting their time. My academic career had ended with a 2.0 GPA at USC *after* taking all of my major courses twice.

"Kevin, look around the room," John said. "How many men do you see here tonight?" Noticing there were about three of us out of the 35 attendees, he saw my confusion.

"How many of these men are your age?" He went on. I was the only one. John said, "We need more people like you, people who are seasoned, have been around the block, and know what they want to do."

By graduation in August 2011, I had passed a probationary class with an A, secured a 3.85 GPA and graduated in the Honors Society as a

Student Marshall. I ended up graduating in August of 2011 as the first class from Regis University with a Masters in marriage and family therapy.

Building My Process

It takes 2,000 hours to become a licensed marriage and family therapist. Most people work for community mental health facilities or agencies at low wages to get hours, free supervision, and benefits at this stage of their career and I was no different. After graduation, I was fortunate to be part of a great team at Arapahoe Douglas Mental Health Network that did crisis intervention and in-home therapy, then worked on the weekends at the Bridge House, which is their acute treatment unit—what most people would call the psych unit. When I was on call, I would have to show up at any one of the hospitals that were in our territory. If a kid called in who was suicidal, homicidal, or psychotic, I would help evaluate them. We would try to figure out whether they needed to go into a full psych hospital or if we could just go into their homes and start doing in-home family therapy.

It was during this time that I learned something crucial: if you change the family system, you can actually change the kid's behaviors.

In my experience, as it turns out, there aren't a lot of 14-year-olds in the world who are truly suicidal or psychotic all by themselves. It generally has more to do with the family system they're engaging with on a daily basis. Because they're so young, kids don't know how to emotionally process everything that's happening in their world. So, they end up saying things like, "I'm going to kill myself," or, "I think I'd rather just not wake up tomorrow." That sounds the alarm bells.

My team started tracking these kids and redirecting them into our outpatient clinic, putting them at the head of the line for psychiatry and for inpatient therapy and outpatient therapy. We would spend three to six weeks going into their houses two or three times a week—helping the whole family understand how to handle things differently or how to diffuse situations. We ended up significantly reducing hospital admissions for these kids. Over 90% of them didn't end up going back into the hospitals and we saved the state a lot of money, in many cases over $100,000 per month. I did that for all of 2012 and 2013, and eventually got burned out on doing trauma and crisis work.

In 2014, I transitioned to a position in a small school district that was primarily Spanish speaking students. I had spent most of my internship working with Spanish speaking families at ADMHN and was often called on to translate for other therapists. We worked it out so that instead of the kids and their families having to come to our offices, I would show up two or three days a week and hang out with the kids at the schools. I really loved this. The school social workers had a list of kids they wanted me to see, so I pulled the kids out of class and we would go hang out—playing soccer, throwing a football, and talking about what's going on. It made a direct impact on them and the school was incredibly grateful.

I met my wife Amy in an AA meeting in Denver that year, and we started dating in February. She owns her own business as an executive search recruiter for the real estate investment trust business. She started suggesting to me that I open up my own practice. Another friend of mine, Dr. James Roman, had been saying the same thing, so I took their advice. I had a panic attack about whether or not I'd actually be able to book my own clients, but quickly found my schedule filling up.

Amy and I ended up getting engaged in January of 2015, bought a house in February, and got married in August of 2016 in Las Vegas by Elvis!

Growth and Change

I started working full-time for myself in August 2014 and have never looked back. I was contacted by my friends Mike Farrell and Cody Gardner, who were running Northstar Transitions in Boulder. They asked me to talk directly to the families and get the parents to take their hands off the kids in treatment—to allow them to start experiencing their own consequences or successes and not have to answer texts, emails, and phone calls 24/7. That launched me into a position where I started seeing about 10 clients a week, engaging with families whose children were in treatment for addiction.

This experience helped me solidify my straight-forward, practical style in terms of how I go about things with the families struggling with addiction and codependency. The irony of life, of course, was that as my relationship with Amy deepened and my practice grew in leaps and bounds, my mother passed away due to her long-term prescription drug use. Her death coupled with the fact that I never got to speak to my step-children or see them again is probably the most painful part of my story.

In 2015, I was contacted by the people who own Aspen Ridge in Lakewood, Colorado. They wanted me to create a two-day family weekend for their program. I did so. It was so successful, that I ended up having to hire about eight or nine contractors. This family weekend ran monthly for four different treatment programs in Colorado for three years. During that time, I continued to see anywhere from 12 to 20 clients a week myself. In 2018, I hired some contract therapists who work for me part time. We do a 70-30 split on their income. I pay for all the expenses and provide the clients; they get 70% of the income.

Things in my life were really starting to trend in a positive direction, and then in April of 2018, my wife and I received some devastating news. My wife went in for a routine colonoscopy and we found out that she had a tumor. Doctors also found that her left kidney was cancerous. They determined that she was going to begin chemotherapy and radiation daily for the next six weeks, then she would need surgery to remove her left kidney and remove the tumor. During all of this, my wife and I had decided we wanted to eventually move to the beach. We had been shopping for places all through the southeast and we ended up landing in Jacksonville Beach in November of 2017.

We looked at the move from Denver to Jacksonville Beach as sort of a pot of gold at the end of the rainbow. I started doing telehealth to see what my client base thought of it, and learned they loved it.

I Can Help

My life has had its ups and downs, but every step brought me closer to understanding how I can help others who are struggling with loved ones who suffer from addiction. First, I was a member of an addicted family, then an addict. I became a sober man, then a sober man with a Master's degree in Marriage and Family Therapy. Both my personal and my professional experiences have furthered my understanding of the impact that addiction and codependency have on family systems.

I am uniquely qualified because of my personal and professional experiences. I have lived all the scenarios – being an addict and recovering, being a caretaker and living in a house of addiction.

I want to help you by sharing my experiences and process, whether you are the addict, the co-dependent, or another mental health professional.

If you have picked up this book, chances are you are already in the throes of dealing with an addict. While you may have discovered your family member uses drugs, tried to set boundaries, and visited countless therapists, you are now at the end of your rope in determining how to change the situation.

I can help.

Over the past 10 years, various methods have worked with clients. But more than that, I think my personal experience with drugs and alcohol has helped families across the nation come to terms with their houses of addiction.

I have a unique perspective on the world that I work in and I also have a reputation as being incredibly direct and straightforward — not dancing around the issues. In grad school, we were taught to be very client-centered and do a lot of active listening and let the client drive the truck and allow them to take the session where they want to take it. I don't do that. My clients come to me because the house is on fire, and they need help putting the fire out. I have a reputation as being a no-nonsense, very direct therapist.

I do not believe in the old tough love approach. My position is: we're going to hold really strong boundaries but we're going to do it with love in our hearts. We're going to say things like, "Kevin, you're my only son and I love you; however, I'm not going to continue to watch you try to kill yourself with drugs and alcohol. I'm going to help you find a solution if you want a solution. If you want to continue to use drugs and alcohol and kill yourself, then I'm going to keep my distance. If you decide you want to get some help, I will do everything in my power to get you help."

That has been my philosophy. I think it's important to tell people you love that they're doing something destructive and potentially lethal, but I think you are also responsible for offering them a solution. Then, you have to let them take the solution or not take the solution. That's up to them.

That was the hardest part about growing up in my family: watching my mom and my dad and their conflict. I tried telling my mom that I thought she had a problem with drugs about five years before she died, and it didn't go very well. I really didn't know what I was doing. I should have gotten some help from the professional. Both she and my dad were very angry with me; my sister kind of had an I-told-you-so attitude that there was no way they were going to hear me or listen to me.

My dad told me to mind my own business, that I didn't know what I was talking about. I couldn't help my parents, but it's not too late for your family. Thank you for picking up this book.

KEY TAKEAWAYS:

- Addiction is characterized by the inability of the addict to control the amount of substance they use and the frequency of their use.

- Addiction is actually more about the addict's life being out of control and unmanageable than the substance abuse.

- Codependency is driven by the agreement that I will work harder on your problem and life than you do.

- Rescuing someone who continues to make poor choices is not called love, it's called enabling. Stop enabling and refuse to be a safety net, so your loved one can grow up.

- I grew up in an addicted home, became an addict, got sober in 1991 and then became a mental health professional.

Part One

Before Treatment

1. Understand that previous actions have been ineffective.

2. Recognize that healing requires an integrated, holistic approach.

3. Work together with the family and set specific goals.

chapter two

TRIAGE YOUR HOME

Chapter 2

Triage Your Home

The first phone call or conversation with many of my stressed, flustered, and panic-stricken clients is usually a derivative of the following:

"Our family member is out of control! We've tried everything! What do we do? I want to bring them to see you. Maybe you can talk some sense into him."

Let's take a step back.

I'd be curious to know what "everything" is you've tried. More importantly, I don't want to see your spouse, parent, or sibling — meaning, I don't want to see just the person who is using drugs or alcohol. Many parents or other family members of someone abusing a substance expect they can simply bring that person to my office in hopes I will revert things back to normal. They are so surprised when I tell them no.

No, I don't want to meet with your addict. I want to meet with *you, the family*. And I want to meet with you alone. There will be plenty of time for family work but first, I want to meet with the management team.

At the first meeting with clients, I reiterate the fact that we're a team. It starts with admitting that the old strategies at home haven't worked and understanding that together, we're going to find a solution that does work. Teamwork starts with an honest answer to the question: "Can we agree that the way you as parents or family members are handling things is not working and that we need to try something new?"

This question isn't designed to make a new client feel defensive or at fault for their family member's addiction or behavior. Rather, family members are responsible for how they *react* to the addiction and behavior. This is true whether the person struggling with an addiction is a teen, a mother, a father, or a sibling.

First, I'll ask about what's been happening at home and within the larger family history. I want the long, detailed history, not the abbreviated, short version with a few data points. This is where I'll ask about the timeline of the substance abuse and how it is impacting the addict and the family.

After hearing the full story, I want to know what the family has already tried. I often learn that the family has spoken to just about everyone in their lives: the family therapist, doctor and psychiatrist, the school counselor and school psychologist, coaches and mentors, the minister, rabbi or priest, and the elders. They have tried everything that was suggested, and still, the family member is drinking, using drugs, and wreaking havoc to their home. The central theme is that the family has to reach outside for expert help, and when they set a hard boundary and hold that boundary no matter what, change is possible. More on this in a moment.

Finally, I ask if the family — every single member, not just the addict — is ready to make real changes. To reiterate, the three main steps in this initial triage process are:

- Gathering the family history and substance abuse timeline
- Learning what the family has tried before

- Asking if everyone is ready to change

- Are you sick and tired of being sick and tired?

Experimenting vs. Abusing

I do not generally work with families in which an individual is *experimenting* with or socially drinking, smoking marijuana, or using other drugs. In these cases, when that individual gets caught at work or at school, they simply need a stern talk and some clear consequences. Nine times out of ten, the non-addict will adjust their behavior accordingly in order to preserve their position or not get kicked out of school.

My process is also not necessarily for a spouse or older parent who receives one DUI and immediately stops drinking. A person facing that kind of problem will get their act together quickly. Minor experimentation (and in most cases, even heavy drinking) can be controlled.

There are three kinds of drinkers: 1) social, 2) heavy, and 3) alcoholics (addicts). For the most part, the techniques I'll be discussing in this book are designed to address those who have an addiction, thought to be between eight and 12% of the population.

This does not include the person who tried some marijuana at a party but didn't try it again, or another person drinking beer with a friend who realizes it isn't her thing. These are instances in which the individual can exhibit self-control. The important thing for you to see: the difference between experimenting and abusing.

A person who is experimenting typically has a good track record and gets caught at home, school, work, or by the police at a party drinking or smoking pot. The critical thing to understand is that people who are experimenting can take it or leave it alone, as they don't feel the need to continue experimenting after they have been caught and experienced the consequences. Their grades stay the same; their work status is not affected; they have the same peer group and friends; and their behavior at home is the same. If this description fits your family member's behavior, then it is likely that the plan described in this book will seem harsh and unfair to you. The key to helping a person who is experimenting is having a family who shows consistency in consequences. Too many times, I see families who apply the consequences periodically rather than consistently, so their loved one then doesn't take them seriously.

It's been my experience, both personally and professionally, that 80 to 90 percent of people who are caught experimenting will generally abide by their family's rules and maybe test their family's tolerance once or twice more.

But the other 10 to 20 percent of people fall into a potential addiction category. These are individuals who continually test the boundaries, hoping their family members will grow tired of trying to hold them accountable with consequences. Some signs to look for if you suspect your family member may be in this category are new friends that are very unlike their old friends, changes in academic or work performance, quitting sports or other activities, and isolating in their rooms when they come home. These are all reasons for you to explain your concern and say, "I love you and if you don't follow the rules, we are going to start drug testing you."

Unacceptable experimentation or abuse begins the moment an individual uses drugs or alcohol *to excess* almost every time they try it. It's likely your family member in this category will be reluctant to tell you the truth about their substance abuse.

If you've seen that your loved one has issues with the law, issues at school or work, and problems at home have started to become a regular occurrence, then they might need my help. While my methods are effective with individuals who are experimenting and those who are abusing, they will probably sound a little drastic to the family of the person who is experimenting. But how do you know if your family member is experimenting or abusing? Or to take it a step further, how do you know if they are experimenting and have the potential to begin abusing?

What is Substance Abuse?

In the 12-Step world of recovery, once a person starts using and cannot control the amount of a substance being used and cannot stop or avoid using, there's a problem. I know that is not what the Diagnostic and Statistical Manual of Disorders, 5th Edition (DSM-5) says, but I like things to be as simple and as direct as possible. Substance abuse is not just about using substances, but also how the substance affects one's life whether one is or isn't using that substance. For the best information on this topic, read the big book of Alcoholics Anonymous and *Codependent No More* by Melody Beattie. Alcoholics Anonymous single handedly revolutionized substance abuse treatment, and its steps work. Before 1935, there was nothing. But now they have an 85-year track record of success.

To determine if there is substance abuse happening in your family, ask yourself: *Is my life or my family member's life unmanageable?* An unmanageable lifestyle involves any of the following:

- Struggles at work or school or getting to work or school
- Issues with maintaining relationships with my friends and family

- Poor time management

- Delinquent financial maintenance or paying bills on time

- Living an unhealthy lifestyle

- Poor hygiene

- Feelings of depression, anxiety, and uselessness

I work with families with members who are tearing up the family and wreaking havoc in their own and others' lives, not the person who is experimenting and can regulate their usage. If you are concerned, look for a change in social circles, grades, work performance, dating patterns, sleep patterns, and any changes in routine. These are some signs that all may not be well with your family member and that it is time for you to intervene and find out what has really been going on. If you think this is your situation, then the course of action I suggest in the following chapters will make a lot of sense to you.

Substance Abuse Denial

There are several phrases I hear from family members who aren't quite ready to admit that Mom, Dad, or Teen may be engaging in substance abuse:

- *"They're just being a teenager,"* or *"It's not a big deal."* Too often, families with an addicted teen come into my office and think their kids are "just being teenagers." This might be true, but these phrases can also be used to mask substance abuse. Somewhere in the past twenty or thirty years, binge drinking has become an acceptable phenomenon in high schools and colleges across the country. "It's just kids blowing off some steam, it's no big deal" is something I hear all too often. Let's be totally clear: binge drinking is extremely dangerous, and it *is* a big deal. Just because your teen can get good grades or is polite at home doesn't mean there's no substance abuse going on. If he or she starts drinking Thursday or Friday night and keeps partying until Monday, there's an issue.

The key ingredient here is the young person's inability to control the amount that is being consumed. Alcoholics talk about how the real problem is the first drink, not the tenth. When you get hit by a train, it's not the caboose that kills you, it's the engine. Pay attention to drinking patterns. Can they just have one beer or one drink or do they almost always get drunk? And remember, if it is your teen you are concerned about, we are not talking about an adult that is drinking legally! If you are supplying the alcohol, you are liable for them and their actions. Is that a risk that you are willing to take?

- *"But he's a functional alcoholic."* I want to be clear with you here, there is no such thing. An alcoholic cannot control the amount they drink. We call that the phenomenon of craving. They also cannot *not* start, even though they know they can't control it. They always come up with a lie or a story or an excuse for why it's okay. We call that the mental obsession. When people say "functional alcoholic," they often mean that the individual in question makes it to work every day. But when I ask them about their relationship with that person, they say, "I hate him," or "I can't trust her." That's not functional.

We use this phrase as a cover story. There's no functionality if you can't *not* start drinking or using substances. Are you having trouble at work? Are you helpful to other people? The truth of the matter is, if someone is an alcoholic, they're not performing as a functional member within the family system. Just because someone goes to work every day does not mean they're managing their life well. It doesn't make them functional. Our society has gotten to the point where money — your ability to earn a paycheck — is more important than your family health, your mental health, your spiritual health, and your emotional health. But it's not. You're just burning the candle at both ends. There is no such thing as a functional alcoholic. Quit giving them a cover story.

- *"It was an accidental overdose."* If someone is doing a drug that they know can kill them, then they are willing to take the chance of dying. There's nothing "accidental" about it; that's just something people say to make family members feel better. The argument will always be, "They were under the influence of the drug, so it's not like they were consciously saying, 'I'm going to shoot heroin today; I may die.'" But that's the whole point of the drug: it takes over and starts making the decisions. That's not an accident. We have to stop making excuses for addiction and start finding solutions. I hate it when people talk about someone that overdosed in the past tense and call it an accident. I always want to ask them, "What did you do to help them stop? Did you ever tell them that you were concerned and offer them a solution?"

- *"It's just pot."* According to the report "Adolescent Cannabis Use: Implications and Treatment Recommendations" by Jennifer Golick, LMFT, who was the Clinical Director of Muir Wood Adolescent & Family Services, marijuana and prescription drugs are the primary substances used by adolescents. Teens who use substances may have lasting cognitive and psychological problems such as deficits in attention, reduced verbal IQ, and reduced executive functioning. Marijuana is incredibly addictive, and using it is a big deal, especially for those with developing brains. Put the brakes on today, or look back in regret five years from now.

Please keep in mind that the potency of marijuana has increased substantially in recent decades. According to Jennifer's report, until the 1990s, the plant had a 2 to 5% concentration of THC. In the early 2000s, it was 8-10%; today it is between 20 and 30%. Signs that a teen is developing Substance Use Disorder include a change in friends, decreasing school performance, change in personality, increased family conflict, disciplinary action in school, abandonment of moral compass, and health or legal problems.

- *"She has deep trauma and uses alcohol to self-medicate."* Yes, people who have deep trauma or deep attachment issues often use drugs and alcohol to self-medicate. But not all of them become addicts and alcoholics. There's a percentage of the population—it's between eight and 12%— that once they start using, they can't control it. These people deserve treatment that works, regardless of the reason they began using.

- *"But he's so smart."* I've heard a lot of alcoholics and addicts say, "This time, it's going to be different, because I'm going to outsmart this." No, you won't. One of the things we say in recovery is, "I've never met anyone too dumb or too stupid to get sober and live a better life; I've met a lot of people that are way too smart." There are a lot of dead smart guys.

- *"They have a prescription."* Just because someone has a prescription from a doctor, doesn't mean they're not engaging in substance abuse. My mother had a prescription but her addiction still ended up killing her.

- *"You don't understand — he's such a good person."* Yeah, I know. I wouldn't doubt that he's a good person…he's probably a *great* person. He's also an addict. People think that if someone has a problem with drugs and alcohol, there's some sort of deep-rooted behavioral problem or character flaw. But that's not it at all. It's more like when an addict tries drugs or alcohol, they just react differently than most people. Think of it like a strawberry allergy. They simply cannot have strawberries. Ever.

Often, I'll hear something from parents like, "He's doing well in school," or "He's going to be a division one athlete! We don't think putting him in treatment is a good idea because it could really hurt his chances." I cringe when I hear this, because when that student goes to college and his team starts drug testing him (like they do), they're going to kick him out. He'll lose that scholarship. Ignoring the problem now doesn't make it go away. But why is their athletic performance more important than their life? My message never changes. The system works but *you* have to work. And the family has to change.

- *"They're going to do what they want to anyway."* This is a big one I hear from adult children when the addict (their parent) is older. My response is, "I hear what you're saying and I get that. It's exactly what I said about my mom. But when you go to your mother's funeral, do you want to be able to look at the casket and say, 'I did everything I could?' Or do you want to have regrets and say, 'I should have done more?'" I ask that question with the families of younger addicts, too.

- *"He'll be mad,"* or *"He'll run away."* It's fine if they're mad. Of course, they'll get mad. And in terms of being afraid to lose him or her, or being afraid your teen will run away, I say, "You've already lost them. It's already happening and you're helping fund it by allowing them to live under your roof and not confronting them. They're off doing what they want anyway." So, let's be honest about what is going on. Take a stand and offer them an opportunity to get sober, to give them a solution. Learning how to say no to your addicted family member is so important. If you can't say no or hold a boundary, you are basically loving that person to death. I don't say any of this to shame or blame; I know how hard this is — you are afraid your family member will die. Finger pointing isn't helpful; I'm all about finding a solution that works. Don't bring a BB gun to a bear fight; we have to hit this disease with everything we've got.

- *"But we need him to work,"* or *"We need her to take care of the kids."* I understand that life and bills don't stop for addiction, and it's a tough situation when your spouse is engaging in substance abuse. But pretending there isn't a problem isn't going to cost less money or time in the long-run. If you don't deal with this problem, your spouse could die. It's that simple.

What I want more people to understand is that addiction is only a little bit about the actual drug or the alcohol. It's much more about the way we live. In the 12 steps, the first step says we're powerless over alcohol, that our lives have become unmanageable. From there, we don't talk about alcohol ever again. The rest of the 12 steps are all about how you need to change the way you live.

There's a phrase we use in the recovery community that I like a lot: "When they're sick and tired of being sick and tired, they're ready to do something different." Another one is, "If nothing changes, then nothing changes." I always ask my clients, "Are you ready to make changes?" I qualify my clients, because if all you want me to do is teach you how to *manage* the family member who is abusing substances better, I cannot help you. So many families think they can just manage the situation. To that, I say, "Okay, we'll put that on his tombstone. We were managing the situation."

Key Triage Assessment Questions

As I mentioned, the first step in working with a family is understanding the family history. The next step is for me to understand the current situation and what has already been tried.

- What kind of substances might your family member be using? Alcohol, drugs, food, gambling and porn all count as addictions. As addictions, they will be the primary focus of this person's time and energy. For example, gaming, when it is an addiction, won't be a fun thing they do with free time, it will be a thing that keeps them out of class and causes them to avoid leaving their gaming system. Food won't be something that they eat because they get enjoyment and nourishment from it, it will be something that controls them, through calorie counting, restricted eating, or binging.

- What has the family already tried? Doctors, therapists, ministers, school counselors? I tend to be the last stop before they give up, so this list can be pretty long.

- Have you sought help for your family member before you picked up this book? If so, who have you turned for help? How many times? What have the responses been?

- A person can be 14, 24, 34, or 64. Their age matters very little when you, as their parent, spouse, sibling, or adult child, are worried about their wellbeing. Things to keep an eye out for: trouble at school, trouble with the law, trouble with the family, and trouble at work.

- The quickest way to find out if your family member is experimenting is to start testing them for drugs and alcohol and see how they react. Apply the consequences immediately and see how they respond.

If you have tried everything and exhausted all of your options as the frustrated family member of an addict, then the solutions I present in this book may be what you have been looking for. Again, I'm not an advocate of the "harm reduction" method used by other therapists in which substance use is simply reduced or managed. I'm here to tell the addict in your family they have to stop using their substance entirely. Forever.

One final thing that is important to understand before we move forward is the difference between a person who is truly sober and what we in the recovery community call a "dry drunk." A dry drunk has quit drinking and using drugs but is not working on their behavior or taking part in any sort of spiritual engagement. All they have done is stop drinking; they haven't changed how they are living, how they're behaving, or how they're treating other people.

When I say that I am sober, I mean I do not take any recreational drugs or alcohol *and* I have a program of recovery. That program of recovery can be anything from faith-based, to meditation and spirituality, 12 steps, yoga, therapy, working out. To reiterate, there are two key ingredients to true sobriety. The first one is that you're totally abstinent from all recreational drugs and alcohol, and the second ingredient is that you have some sort of discipline or plan regarding how you're changing the way you live, the way you act, and the way you treat other people.

KEY TAKEAWAYS:

- People who are experimenting don't feel the need to continue experimenting with drugs or alcohol after they have been confronted and experienced the consequences.

- Individuals who are abusing cannot control the amount of a substance being used and cannot stop or avoid using. Often, they show signs of trouble with the law, friends, family, school, or work.

- It's critical to address the family system as a means to help the person who is struggling with addiction and unmanageability.

- When a company is struggling, you address the management team first and then the employees, not the other way around. What this means in this context is the entire family will have to change.

- You are not responsible for your family member's addiction; you are responsible for how you react to it.

- A sober person has stopped using drugs and alcohol and has a plan to change the way they live, the way they act, and the way they treat other people. Someone that just stopped using drugs and alcohol but has not changed the way they live and act is called "Dry."

WORKSHEET

1. What is the full family history?

Let's say the person engaging in substance abuse is your husband.

Have you talked to his parents?

_____

Have you talked to his brothers and sisters?

_____

When did this start?

_____

When my clients come to me and say, "This just happened a couple years ago," I say, "That's just not how it works." Tell the full story.

_____

_____

_____

2. What have you tried already?

Who have you talked to?

_____

Have you tried therapy?

_____

Have you tried the leadership of your faith-based community?

_____

Have you tried talking to the individual?

_____

Have you played all your cards?

_____

3. Timeline:

What is the timeline of the drug and alcohol use?

_____

Has it gotten better or has it gotten worse?

_____

Is the marriage in jeopardy?

_____

Is the job in jeopardy? School? Grades?

_____

Is access to the kids in jeopardy?

_____

Have they started to lose friends? Has their social life gotten better or worse?

4. Are you ready?

Do you have any reservations? Do you still think that they're going to pull out of this nosedive all by themselves? There isn't a therapist on the planet that can get someone sober. The whole family has to be ready to make major changes. Because when I say "sober," I'm not talking about quitting using drugs and alcohol. I'm talking about quitting drugs and alcohol and living a new way of life.

_____

_____

_____

_____

_____

_____

DESIGNING PLAN A: BOUNDARIES, ACCOUNTABILITY, AND CONSEQUENCES

Chapter 3

Designing Plan A: Boundaries, Accountability, and Consequences

As a parent, spouse, sibling or adult child of someone abusing a substance, you likely feel one (or several) emotions: frustration, anger, or hopelessness. Your family members may be sitting around a table, blaming one another for what has gone wrong. And you may be thinking to yourself: *This is my fault. What did I do wrong?*

First, accept that this is not your fault. And second, know that you're not alone. It's not your fault that your family member likes to use drugs and alcohol. Even if that family member happens to be your child.

As kids grow more resourceful, they will find whatever substances they want if they want them.

You can be the most loving, kind supportive person on the planet and still end up dealing with your family member's substance abuse issues. Addiction is not a result of anything you have done wrong or right. It doesn't matter if the individual was breast-fed or bottle-fed, nurtured and given every opportunity available. It doesn't matter if you were the perfect spouse or ideal sibling. Addicts make up about 10 percent of the population. Addiction is biological. In other words, if you have addiction in your family, you've got it. Think of it like being pregnant, you either are or you aren't.

Addiction isn't something that someone can pick up in a public restroom, or by hanging out with the "wrong crowd," or from watching too much MTV, or from going to a work happy hour. Addicts come from all walks of life regardless of their faith, socio-economic background, education level, race, creed, color, or sexual orientation. We call it the equal opportunity disease.

Your Responsibility

Your responsibility as a family member is how you react to the fact that your loved one is abusing substances. Making significant improvements to this person's life starts with setting up a system and addressing the way your family engages and interacts with one another, thus holding every family member accountable.

Creating a family dynamic that has clear boundaries and expectations will allow you to deal with whatever adversity comes your way. Remember, you're not responsible for your family member's addiction but you are responsible for how you respond to it. You can learn to live with an addict who is active in their addiction, or is sober. You do not have to let them run the show with all the drama, crisis, and chaos that comes with substance abuse.

I've been there. I understand all of the perspectives, so my recommended solutions are based upon my experience of having been in the family, being active in addiction, being sober and being a mental health professional.

Consistency, accountability, and transparency are three critical elements of a successful resolution to substance abuse and codependency.

And these components aren't just for the addict, but for the entire family system as well.

Setting boundaries, accountability measures, and rewards and consequences are three important components to addressing your family member's addiction to drugs and alcohol, and your dysfunctional family system. The individual's addiction often has an effect on work, academics, or behavior at home. This relationship between addictions and external behavior can take on different forms. Often a person's work life or academics and behavior at home may be fine, but partying is out of control. Or maybe behavior at home hasn't been an issue, but the drugs and alcohol are causing problems with work or family finances. Any of these situations can lead to trouble for both you and for the whole family.

Boundaries

Start drawing lines. That's what a boundary is. The most important thing you as the family member of an addict can understand about boundaries is that boundaries aren't about the addict. They are about you. Boundaries are about you saying, "Enough!" and sticking to it.

Boundaries set parameters, letting the other person know what you will and will not tolerate. While we often use boundaries throughout our everyday lives, it is equally important to create and maintain a boundary with your family member. Especially when the addict is your child, you are the parent in this situation. Both you and your kids need to understand and respect that dynamic.

An example of establishing boundaries in your home can include any of the following:

1. No using drugs or alcohol ever.
2. In our house we have the expectation of either consistent work (with a regular paycheck) or attendance at school and maintaining a 3.0 GPA.
3. In our family. we do not use threats. We do now allow hitting, lying, or yelling at one another. We use "please," "thank you," and "excuse me" when we are speaking to one another.

Accountability

Clients have often told me, "I have tried to set a boundary before, but my husband doesn't ever follow it." My question is always, "Did you enforce any level of accountability?"

Accountability means you've established a consequence or counter-measure for activating that boundary if it isn't followed properly.

For example, if a teen is drinking or using drugs and the parents tell me, "We've told him no more drugs and alcohol, but he does it anyway," I say, "Great. Let's start doing drug tests." They will often respond with, "He knows how to beat them."

Your loved one doesn't know how to beat a hair follicle test. He might be able to scam a urine test or a breathalyzer, but there is no way to trick a hair follicle test for drugs. Also, when you use a breathalyzer and a urine test on a consistent basis, your loved one might be able to fool it once or twice. But eventually, the tests will tell the truth. Yes, the cost of a drug test is always a factor. But remember: car accidents, therapeutic boarding schools, treatments, and funerals are even more expensive.

If the addict is your spouse and you don't want to be in charge of drug testing, the accountability piece could take the form of your spouse having to go get a lab test on their own every week. Or you could have them use a tool like SoberLink®, which is a tamper-resistant device an individual can blow into for real time alcohol monitoring results.

You've created a boundary.

Now be accountable for it.

Boundaries without any accountability are a waste of time — both to you and to the addicted family member. For example, let's say that you are driving down the street. The boundary that's set for you is a speed limit of 35 miles per hour, but you speed past a cop, driving at 100 miles per hour. Rather than turning on his lights and immediately pulling you over, the cop just waves — there is no accountability! It doesn't matter if you broke the law, drove over the speed limit, and risked hurting yourself or anyone else. However, if the cop is there with a radar gun to hold you accountable and you drive over the accepted limit, she will pull you over and give you a ticket. You need to hold your family member accountable in the same fashion.

What you are doing by setting boundaries and enforcing them through accountability and structure is the same thing. You are teaching your family member how to be responsible, and how to take responsibility for their behavior. These are often the biggest complaints that the family members of addicts have: they don't have accountability or any level of responsibility.

Exactly. Because you don't hold that person accountable. You take care of everything and allow your child, spouse, sibling or parent to make excuses for falling short or failing drug tests. Why should your family member show any level of responsibility for their actions if there's no accountability?

Rewards and Consequences

Rewards and consequences are the final piece of Plan A. For example, the family members of an addicted individual set the boundary: No drugs and alcohol. Then accountability comes in when you start breathalyzing the loved one, along with administering weekly drug tests. Consistent rewards and consequences are the final step to this regimen. If the addict doesn't pass the drug test and shows positive results, the family then takes away their access to regular family life (if the addict is an adult) or their social life (if the addict is a teen) until they do pass the tests. If they pass the tests, then all privileges are restored.

Consistency is critical during this step as success is created through repetition.

Yes, there will be anger. To follow this particular example, I'd be surprised to learn if your loved one wasn't upset by this. At the extreme, he may run out the door. If the addict is a teen, the parent can then call the police and say, "I need to report my kid. He's gone. He's missing curfew, and we had this debate about drugs and alcohol."

The response I often get from the parents of an addicted teen is, "But then my kid will have a criminal record!" May I remind you: if your teen is an addict, they might get a criminal record as a minor but the legal consequences are much less severe than when they're an adult. Occasionally, the cops will bring your kid home or ask you to come get pick him up. If your kid continues to cause this problem, they will end up getting a record, but at 18 years of age, that record will be sealed.

If you are the parent of an addict, wouldn't you rather your child deal with addiction in the early teen years than at 18, 19, and 20 years old? At those older ages, an entirely different set of rules comes into play.

Rewards and Consequences for Adult Addicts

This piece of the Plan A equation looks a bit different when the addict is your spouse or parent. It may take the form of access to your children. This would involve you saying to your spouse or parent, "If you are not drinking and not using drugs and can pass the test, you get access to the kids."

If your spouse is an addict and you've already kicked them out of the house, you can offer a pretty simple reward — being able to return home. But if you're still living with your addicted spouse, the reward might be: "If you pass every drug test, you can stay here and sleep in the big bed. If you can't, then there's the door."

It has to be that black and white. The door has to slam on their fingers. If the addict is the one who owns the house, fine. Pick up the kids and leave. Go stay at a hotel, go stay at a friend's or at a family member's house. That's why the last question in the previous chapter is so important. Are you ready to make it happen? No more messing around. If you're ready to make a move, to get serious, it may require you having to move out of your home. You may have to take the kids, file for divorce, file for a separation, get a temporary restraining order. Are you ready for these things? A lot of these questions may involve a lawyer. Talk to one.

Yes, Plan A might be more challenging when you are dealing with your spouse instead of your teen, but that doesn't mean you can't implement it. Go back to the basics. When we talk about addiction, what we're talking about is one question: is the person powerless over the drug or the alcohol? Does the drug or the alcohol make the decisions? The quick way to find out is to simply ask them to quit using for the next two weeks or a month. See how it goes. If you get a bunch of stories and static, as in, "I don't need to and I don't have to," you've got your answer. People who don't have addiction can walk away without any issues when the people they love ask them to. Period.

If your spouse clearly cannot stop smoking pot every day, for example, we roll into the process of instituting boundaries, accountability, and rewards and consequences. The boundary is no drugs, the accountability is drug testing. He might say, "I'm not doing it," or start lying and trying to cheat the test. That's fine. Create the structure to watch how people behave. This gives us the baseline of how they're responding to a hurdle, a change in the system. Rewards and consequences are then really straightforward: "If you can't get sober, then we need to talk about whether or not we're going to stay married."

Another boundary can be around work, school, treatment, or regular therapy. You can say, "I need you to go to individual therapy and I'd like to do couples therapy." You don't need to know what he is discussing in those sessions, but you need evidence he went. If his answer is no, then you can say, "Okay, then we can't stay together."

Spouses of addicts always say some version of, "But you said I can't manage them!" But you're not managing. You're talking about how things are make-or-break and holding them accountable. Whether they do it or not is totally up to them. You are just holding your boundaries.

Talk about the addict's behavior at home. Is he present for you? Present for the kids? Is he swearing in front of the kids and at the kids? Have a weekly therapy meeting where you sit down and talk about all that stuff regarding how the week went. It's really a very black and white system. I work with people in that space; I don't work with people who are dipping their toes in the water or just hoping to reduce their spouse's drug use. You've got to want to *change*. Big, lasting change. My process is for when you've been through the meat grinder and are done playing the game, done fighting, done chasing your tail and done with the fantasy that they are going to wake up tomorrow and suddenly realize all of the damage that they have done. The only way we're going to impact change on the individual is if we change the entire system. If the system no longer accepts a behavior, it will change.

This system also works when the addict doesn't live with you. I was 27 years old when my family used this approach with me. Basically, I was told I was out of the family, that there would be no contact while I was actively using drugs or alcohol. But here's the important part: They also said, "If you want help, we will help you get help. But until that time, the answer is no."

And it saved my life.

Family members always think that while an addict is using and the family system is spinning out of control that it's their job to sit there and endure the beating. And it's not. One of the first things I always say is, "You don't have to put up with that crap. You can choose to walk away and tell them, 'Until this changes, I'm not coming back.'"

Real-World Situations with Teens

What if your situation at home has gone to the extreme? Since I work with a lot of parents whose teens have a substance use problem, I'm going to devote a few pages here to things I've seen and suggestions I have around this particular situation. Understand that setting boundaries and holding your son or daughter accountable is actually creating a safe environment for them. The fascinating thing is kids often want and respond well to boundaries. While no kid wakes up thinking: *Wow, I wish my parents would hold me accountable and have more boundaries*, when there aren't any boundaries and there isn't any accountability, kids panic because there isn't any consistency.

I have seen family after family begin holding boundaries around substance use, academics, and behavior. From that one crucial step, the change that occurs is miraculous and almost immediate. Once kids know where the lines are, what the consequences are and that they will be applied consistently, they have a sense of predictability in their home. This helps them learn how to use these elements in their lives and create emotional regulation. Kids like their lives to be predictable; it makes them feel safe and allows them to grow emotionally and mature. When they don't know what will happen next, things can get really chaotic. The boundary you set is about saying to them, "I love you so much that I am not going to accept this behavior anymore. I am not going to tolerate this. This is not okay with me."

The most important part about boundaries is that they cannot be done punitively. Setting boundaries is not done with guilt, shame, finger pointing, or arguing. It's done with love and compassion. For example, you may say: "Ben, I love you. I am no longer willing to accept your using drugs and alcohol. It's because I love you and I care about you. It's also not negotiable. It isn't a debate. I am telling you as your father that this is no longer acceptable. The way we are going to enforce is through consistent drug tests and breathalyzers. We will start by taking you to a facility and completing an initial drug test, so we have a baseline which will tell us which drugs you are using and how much you are using them."

It is critical to start with a baseline number for the drug use so you can measure over time and see if your loved one has actually stopped using or continues to use. It also sets the precedent that you are not making idle threats. You mean business.

I don't engage with the 16-year old drug user. I engage with that teen's parents. After all, the change starts with the parents. I do encourage the parents to find a therapist for their kid and have individuals on my staff who are amazing with adolescents, teens, and young adults. As a matter of fact, that's why I hired them!

Disagreements Among Family Members

When I explain boundaries, accountability, and consequences, and families mention they've tried that approach before, I'll ask what happened when their loved one tested positive for drugs. The result I often hear is something like, "We couldn't agree on what to do, and we weren't on the same page."

This is where the whole system can fall apart. If you don't take substance abuse seriously, then how can you expect your loved one to take it seriously? Write down what the boundaries are and what the accountability will look like: No drug use, and regular testing. From there, together, we move on to the third piece of this puzzle, which is the rewards and consequences element: if your loved one tests positive for drugs, rewards will get taken away. In the case where the addict is a teen, that would mean things like access to the car or to their phone. In the case where the addict is an adult, being part of the family and being able to stay in the family home is the reward.

Families always say the same thing to me at this point, in cases where the addict is a teen: "We tried taking his phone, but he won't give it to us." Let's address this excuse head-on. Whose phone is it, actually? If your kid does not pay the bill, the phone belongs to the parents. If you need to, you as a parent can reach out to your service provider and have the phone number removed from your plan or the service limited to only a few numbers. Or, you can turn off the data plan and change the wireless password at the house. Another option: you can shut the phone off and get them an old-fashioned flip phone. There is nothing more humiliating to a teenager than having a flip phone.

Devices can be tricky. They often require you changing the Wi-Fi password to enforce the boundaries you've set. Most Wi-Fi providers have a router available that will allow you to shut down specific devices. If you need to employ this, do so. When I say, "Take away your kid's phone," I mean take away all of the electronics – the iPad, the PlayStation, the Xbox. All of those devices can access the internet. No TVs, no computers. Take everything away.

Technology for Schoolwork

What if the addict in the family is your teen who does their schoolwork on a computer, as most of them do now? No problem: have them complete their homework in front of you. While monitoring their screen time, allocate a certain amount of time for them to complete homework, and if it's not done, then it's not done. That is your kid's fault and your kid's problem. Hold them accountable.

This leads to the second boundary with accountability when the addict in your family is a student: academics. You are going to ask your kid's teachers for a weekly report on behavior and academics. Engage in emailing all of your kid's teachers, the principal, the school counselors, and the school psychologist. Tell them your therapist said this is what you need to do, and that you need their help. It is generally very easy to get this started. At this point, your kid becomes responsible for showing up at home on Friday afternoons with something from each of the teachers. This is either achieved or it's not. If it is not achieved, then your kid will spend the weekend doing their homework and chores. Once it is done, then you can start talking about some freedom and rewards, such as access to devices or time with friends.

Incentivize Good Behavior

Let's stay with an example in which your addicted loved one is your teen. I like things that are very tangible, so sometimes the incentive you offer your loved one can be that they get to use their cell phone, get access to the internet, or get access to the car and a social life. Those are three fantastic incentives, and ones that they will likely respond to. Another is that they get a social life. If your teen can pass a drug test you administer, keep up their academic progress, and behave well at home, they can have all of those things. Obviously, you want to continue to positively incentivize good behavior.

You can even choose to go long-term with your incentives and tell your teen, "If the drug test stays clean, you can get that GPA up to a 3.5, and you get your five hours a week of chores done, we would be open to this, this, and this." The reward might be a certain vacation or a summer camp they're interested in.

At this point, I'm a big fan of bringing the addicted member of your family into the conversation and asking, "What do *you* want?" They might say, "I want to get high," but that's not going to happen. It is never an incentive. Drugs and alcohol are never an acceptable incentive.

I am very task and goal-oriented, as well as direct and straightforward. I will always ask my clients what their goal is. What is the goal with the drugs and alcohol? What's the goal with academics? What's the goal at home? If you are uncomfortable with setting and reinforcing these boundaries, why? Ask a few questions of yourselves as parents: Do you not trust each other? Do you not rely on each other? What's the story?

Inevitably, in cases where the addicted family member is a teen, one parent is being what we call a "helicopter parent," hovering over the kid and constantly taking care of things. Often in this situation, the other parent is the drill sergeant. When this is the case, it is because this dynamic is usually familiar to how the parents were raised as well, so they are recreating a home environment based on what they know and what they have seen.

Deeper Family Dynamics

Deeper family dynamics and issues are often a key component to addiction. Once we arrest the behavior pattern of the person abusing the substance, then we can work not just with the individual who is struggling with substances, but we can start talking about how the family is responding to the situation and why. We can start to dig in and do the interesting family-of-origin work with the parents. I look to identify the history of substance abuse and mental health issues. We talk about what it was like in their household growing up and why they struggle with their ability to hold a kid accountable.

Once we get our initial plan in place for drugs and alcohol, academics, and behavior at home, often a deeper family dynamic issue starts to come out. Why aren't you able to hold your loved one accountable for their substance abuse? What's really going on there? Essentially, we are triaging the entire family at this point in the process. When it comes to more personal issues, however, I generally refer clients to other therapists that are more engaged in processing than I am.

The alcoholic's problem is simple, really: stop using. Just stop. Stop sitting in the basement playing video games; get a job. They're easy, because they know that what they are doing is destructive. They know.

Often, the behavior of the rest of the family is more complex and takes longer to untangle because they tell a story that what they are doing is right or helpful when it's not. Families build these generational layers of systems ingrained in keeping the family the way it is.

The family members have *invested their lives* in enabling and accommodating the addict. When they don't have to do that anymore, a lot of things come up around identity and loss of control. Often, the enabler is terrified of having their role taken away, because now they don't have any power. Consider the mom who sees her role as controlling her kid's life and telling everybody, "I've got it all handled!" She's spinning the plates, like the old vaudeville act. When I tell her to drop the plates, she doesn't want to do it, because then she won't have a job. When I can start to really see and understand what's going on in the hearts and the minds of the family members, then I can truly understand how to help.

We can start to make really huge strides on the changes when we can start to see the family system and the generational layers of the family system. The spouse of an alcoholic, for example, will begin to reveal what it was like for her as a kid (because it wasn't an accident that she ended up married to an addict). Is there a lack of self-esteem on her part? Why? We'd start digging into that stuff. Again, healthy families are created by healthy individuals and healthy individuals work on their stuff.

We've created this belief in America that you're functional or dysfunctional; you're healthy or unhealthy. That kind of thinking is just not helpful. People refuse to admit to having addiction or mental illness in their families because they're afraid they'll immediately get painted with a broad brush: "the crazy people."

The stigma is total crap. Everybody has stuff. Everybody. And if we could get to a point, as a country, where we actually acknowledge that and understand there is no perfect family, we'd be a lot better off. Everybody needs help. Everyone has a little bit of depression, a little bit of anxiety. I don't care who you are. It's about how you deal with it that matters.

Nothing to Lose

A corporation has a set of rules and regulations. If they find somebody drunk on the job, they implement a process. They have a plan: "You have a problem? We're going to put you into the system." My role as a therapist is to coach families into a process that works: to show them how to apply it, and listen to them as feelings arise. My clients will often say about their loved one, "Oh my God, he's going to be so mad if I say I'm going to drug test him. I feel so guilty." I say, "I understand. Let's talk about that some more. Why do you feel guilty?"

One of the things that I always come back to is the way your family member is dealing with things now — using drugs or alcohol — isn't great. He's killing himself. So, what have you got to lose by implementing Plan A? At the very least you're giving him an opportunity to change his behavior. My clients say, "If we do this, it'll drive him out on the street and he'll just start shooting heroin."

I want to be clear with you. He's already doing that. Now you're offering him an alternative.

KEY TAKEAWAYS:

- You're not responsible for your family member's addiction, but you are responsible for how you respond to it.

- Boundaries, accountability, and consequences or rewards are important components to resolving your family member's addiction to drugs and alcohol.

- Boundaries are about you, not the addict. You have to be willing to set them and hold them. It is not a negotiation.

- Accountability is how you are going to hold the boundaries; what system of accountability are you going to use?

- The final piece of Plan A is a consequence or a reward for following the boundaries and the accountability.

- Setting boundaries and holding your family member accountable is actually creating a safe environment for them.

- When the addict is a teen, it's critical for both parents to agree on boundaries, accountability, and consequences or rewards.

- For the addict to change, the entire family has to change.

WORKSHEET

I've put my suggestions (examples) in italics. Customize these to your family. Remember, these are not to be negotiated or argued about with the addict.

Boundaries

Let's say the person engaging in substance abuse is your husband.

Drugs and Alcohol: *None*

School or Work: *Regular school or work attendance. GPA 3.0 or above; regular pay check*

Behavior at Home: *No hitting, no yelling, no lying, no cheating. Chores get done*

Accountability

Let's say the person engaging in substance abuse is your husband.

Drugs and Alcohol: *Regular testing*

School or Work: *Regular paycheck or regular school progress reports, evidence of attendance. It is the student's job to provide this*

Behavior at Home: *Family meeting or family therapy to review the list of how the week went, if boundaries were honored*

Rewards and Consequences

1. *Access to mobile and/or gaming devices*

2. *Access to the car*

3. *Access to the kids*

4. *Being part of the family*

5.

6.

7.

8.

9.

10.

GETTING STARTED: IMPLEMENTING PLAN A

Chapter 4

Getting Started: Implementing Plan A

By choosing this book, you realize your family member is not simply experimenting with drugs or alcohol, and actually needs help. While experimenting with drugs or alcohol is not necessarily acceptable, it is a common behavior. If you are one of the few lucky people who have had a kid, parent, sibling or spouse admit they have used a few substances and didn't like them, and you are not seeing any significant changes in that family member's behavior or performance in school or work, then you likely don't need to follow the suggested recommendations outlined in the next few pages. Generally, after asking them to take a weekly drug test, the person that experiments will not use again and the tests will show this. (*Note: this chapter focuses on alcohol and marijuana. Please turn to Chapter 5 for a deeper focus on other harder drugs*).

In doubt about whether your family member has progressed beyond basic experimentation? Consider creating, implementing and sticking to a plan equipped with concrete boundaries, accountability, and rewards and consequences. One of the easiest ways to determine if a person has progressed beyond basic and normal experimentation is by identifying changes in that individual's performance in school or work, their social circle, and interests.

The second easiest way is simply asking your family member to take a drug test. As a general rule, people who are not abusing drugs or alcohol don't complain when asked to complete a drug test. But if your family member is using, expect them to complain, deny using drugs, and attempt to find a way to beat the test. They may also accuse you of not trusting them or not loving them. One of my favorite quotes about addiction is helpful here. It comes from Dr. Kevin McCauley, founder of The Institute for Addiction Study and the creator of the excellent film *Pleasure Unwoven*: "Addiction begins as a disorder of genes and pleasure and ends as a disorder of choice." Our job with Plan A, then, is to deeply and permanently interrupt the choice to use drugs and alcohol before it progresses.

To do so, the family of an addicted person must help that person to stop taking drugs and consuming alcohol, learn to cope with craving, manage stress, and participate in recovery every day. The result of this work, according to Dr. McCauley, is "the power of choice is restored...and normal pleasures become pleasurable again." I highly recommend watching *Pleasure Unwoven* for an insightful look from an expert in the field on how to better understand the disease of addiction.

You've Set the Boundary. Now Be Accountable for It

Holding a loved one accountable to your "no drugs or alcohol" boundary starts with a drug test, either at a professional facility or at home. Choosing a twelve-panel drug test ensures comprehensive testing for as many drugs as possible. If you're purchasing an at-home test, choose one that will test temperature, content, and water level of urine. Testing temperature is important because if your family member is using someone else's urine to beat the test, it won't be warm. Testing the water level of urine is critical because drinking copious amounts of water just before a test can dilute urine.

One of the easiest ways to work around the test is by using someone else's urine, but a local testing facility has on-site professionals who will watch your family member take the test. And don't forget, you can also have your family member take multiple drug tests at random times and avoid telling him or her when they're going to receive a drug test, so there's minimal time for them to prepare for the test.

As an example, if you wake your family member at six in the morning, it's hard to prepare enough to fake the test. Or after an initial session at my office, I often tell clients to stop at the local pharmacy on the drive home, purchase a twelve-panel test and watch their family member urinate in the cup. Don't be shy about sitting in the bathroom and watching them fill the cup. If this really bothers you, then take your family member to the local facility and have a professional handle it.

Regardless, if you believe your loved one is trying to work around a urine drug test, skip to a hair follicle test at a local facility. A hair follicle test indicates drug or alcohol use up to 90 days prior to the test. These tests are extremely accurate and impossible to cheat.

Several brands of hair follicle tests are available on Amazon and other online retailers. While a urine test will show immediate results, a hair follicle test will take more time. An advantage to visiting a local facility is that the team will provide results immediately, plus email the results in greater detail several days later. These results can indicate approximately how much and how often each drug has been used.

Do you think your loved one is drinking? Purchase a breathalyzer and use it regularly. Test your family member before and after they come home or whenever you feel it is necessary. Basic breathalyzers are also available on Amazon for around $100. There is an amazing device called a SoberLink® that looks like a mobile phone and takes a picture every time a person takes a test. The SoberLink® can be set to go off multiple times a day and you cannot beat it. You either submit a positive or a negative test at the designated time or you don't and an alert is sent to whoever is monitoring the client.

Drug and alcohol testing can sound expensive, but a few hundred dollars spent on testing and intervening into your family member's addiction now is only a fraction of the cost of inpatient treatment, which can be up to $30,000 per month.

The Results Are In. Now What?

If your family member passes the drug test, allow them access to the family (in cases where the addict is your spouse, parent, or sibling). If the family member is your kid, allow them access to their phone, internet, social life, car and any other privileges that you, as a parent, are comfortable providing.

If your family member does not pass the drug test, enforce the consequences. Do not provide any privileges until they do pass the test.

What if the test results come back unclear? Refusal to take another test or unclear results is considered a positive result. After all, if someone is actively avoiding a drug test, it's likely they are trying to hide something.

I understand this firm Plan A approach isn't easy to implement. But you can do it, and I know it works. I recently asked one of my clients about her experiences working together to provide some perspective. She initially came to me regarding her son's substance abuse and ultimately addressed her own issues with drugs and alcohol as well. This is what she had to say about our time together: "It's not just talking. Kevin expects you to do your own work. You go to Al-Anon, find a sponsor, work the steps. I was just as sick if not more so than my son. [Kevin] expects you to do your own work and doesn't have a lot of leeway for excuses. You have a responsibility to yourself and your children."

This client also mentioned that I don't let my clients get away with lying or giving me excuses, which is true. But I approach everything I do with compassion and first-hand experience with addiction. She continued, "He calls it like it is but is very nurturing. He has a lot of resources and uses his experience to relate to the world of addiction. It is very dangerous for a parent to seek counseling from anyone outside the addiction world. You need someone who has lived it to be able to say, 'That is not okay,' as addiction is a *life and death disease.* Anyone that is dealing with addiction must seek a counselor that specializes in addiction.

"I will lose more people to addiction than I will ever lose to COVID. It's *that* critical, *that* important. A lot of people think they can send their child to rehab and it's their problem. But addiction is a family disease, a generational disease. I wish more people would look at it that way. We'd have less death, more peace."

This particular client of mine saw addiction impact five generations of her family. Part of it is the fact that addiction is in your DNA (meaning, it has a strong genetic component), but part if it is learned codependency and enabling passed down from parent to child, over and over. Families often keep saving the addicted individual and bailing them out to their own detriment.

There is this myth of the addict living under the highway overpass, but that's not the truth. This client's family, for example, had tons of money and looked very shiny from the outside (as she puts it), yet had a lot of dysfunction going on. Fortunately, the pattern will stop with her and with her son because of the difficult work they did and are still doing.

"Kevin saved my life, he really did," she says. "He made me work my ass off. But I would not be where I am without him. He knows who to call, he knows all the players. In this world, there are some really bad actors, bad programs. But he knows the best places out there, taking into account your situation."

Improve Performance at School or Work

You've seen the test results, and now it's time to get your family member's performance at school or work back on track. When my family started holding me accountable, for example, they wanted to see proof that I was actually doing what it took to earn my college degree.

It's unrealistic to demand perfection in your family member, but it *is* realistic to expect good performance at school or work, meaning a regular paycheck or good attendance, good grades, and good behavior. Set clear expectations with your loved one about what their job is right now:

receiving a good education if they are your child; earning a living to pay rent or contribute to family bills if they are an adult.

Once you have determined what your expectations are and shared them with your family member, start using boundaries, accountability and rewards and consequences. For example, if the addict is your teen, draw a firm line that their GPA should be at a 3.0 or better. Integral to this boundary is that they should not have missing assignments for any class and should have good attendance. It is their responsibility to give you proof of this.

If the family member in question is your spouse, the boundary here is simply a regular paycheck.

Hold your loved one accountable for meeting these boundaries by having them engage with their education or work. Stay abreast of their performance through weekly reports from each teacher or biweekly paychecks. Making your family member accountable for their education or their job teaches responsibility.

Rewards and Consequences

If your family member is meeting your boundaries, they can have access to all privileges. If the boundaries are not achieved, show consistency and systematically remove their privileges. Remove all of them at once, if the performance is particularly bad.

You can hold the people you love accountable — at any age — and say, "We're going to address the drugs and alcohol. You've got to address work or school. Then, we've got to address the way everyone behaves within the structure of the family."

You also have to provide them with a solution, as in, "We'll help you find someone who can help, whether it's a therapist or treatment. We will help you there." In my case, it looked more like, "Oh, you didn't graduate from college? Okay, we will help you. I'm not saying we'll pay for it. I'm saying we'll help you map out a path where *you're* going to take care of it."

The last key piece, of course, is for everyone to be engaged as a part of this family. These are the things that have to happen. Plan A is: "We'll help you, but we ain't gonna do it for you and we're not going to accept the way things are."

The old school tough love approach was: "You got to quit drinking and doing drugs. Until then, don't call me. We're locking you out of the house; we're going to pretend like you don't exist until you take care of it." Tough love slams the door on their fingers, turns your back on them and acts like they don't exist. It's very shame-based.

My approach is firm, but more compassionate. what I propose is more along the lines of, "Hey, we're afraid you're going to kill yourself, and we're afraid you're going to die and so we want that to change. And until you buy in, we're not going to participate. So, we're going to let you start feeling the consequences of your behaviors and your actions." But we're also going to say, "If you want help, we have secured it for you, and we're happy to give you the help, but you have to buy in."

When I was an active addict, my family held me accountable by holding their ground. They had done this before and always caved in. But when I was 27, they held the line and caught my attention. Now I have 29 years of sobriety. When you don't have access to your family and they're not returning your phone calls and they're not spending time with you, that will get your attention. I had a job, I was paying my bills, I didn't need them financially, but I still needed them. Which is why my program works no matter the age of the family member.

The family simply has to say, "These are the terms. These are the conditions. You're putting your life at risk and that has to stop. We love you. We're here to help you."

First, you have to *eliminate the drugs and the alcohol.* Nothing else matters. Once that's eliminated, then we can start worrying about the "why" and about the family dynamics. People always want to go at it from the other perspective of, "Let's figure out what the problem is and why he uses so much, maybe that will help him moderate how much he uses."

And it just doesn't work.

You are out of the addict management business. Put out the fire first by saying "No drugs, no alcohol."

Improving At-Home Behavior

- **Boundaries:** Setting boundaries at home can be fairly basic, such as: no foul language, no bullying, no violence, no property damage, having all chores done correctly and on time, and speaking respectfully to all family members. Remember that these boundaries apply to everyone, not just kids. If you want your children to be respectful of you, then you need to lead by example. People learn by example, no matter how old they are, so provide them with an example of how you want to be treated. Modeling behavior goes for both good and bad behavior, so remember you are modeling what you would like to see.

- **Accountability:** This can be as easy as starting a weekly family meeting to review everyone's behavior. But if you are unsure how to structure the discussion, start this process in a weekly family therapy session.

- **Rewards and consequences:** If all of the boundaries are met (drugs/alcohol, school/work and behavior at home), then your family member regains access to the home and family. If we are talking about a teen here, then all of their at-home privileges are restored. If the boundaries are not met, then remember consistency: restrict privileges or family access until the next family meeting. Let your family member know that this is how you are going to handle things from here forward. No more arguing, fighting, bargaining or threats. You are going to host a simple meeting at the end of the week when everyone is going to review all the boundaries and see how it's going. Facts are facts, and no one can argue with drug tests, school report cards, the presence or absence of paychecks, and family meetings.

A common thread with developing a plan to stop your family member's addiction and improve their performance at school or work and at-home behavior, is to take action. After setting your boundaries, hold everyone involved accountable for their actions, including yourself.

Real-world situation: Learning disabilities or poor time management skills

If your family member is struggling with school or work due to a learning disability or poor time management, help them. Learn how your loved one can receive support at work or at school, for example, with a 504 or an Individualized Education Plan (IEP) if someone has a learning disability or social emotional issues that prevent them from doing well.

If your family member is showing poor time management, ask them to show you what they're learning or what they're expected to do at work and how they problem-solve. Sounds time-consuming, right? It is, but your family member is your top priority. If the addict in your family is your child, teaching them how to be a better student leads to success; if the addict is your spouse, helping them better manage their time will help keep them employed. However, avoid completing homework or work assignments for your loved one, or allowing them to blow off responsibilities. Time management skills are critical to success.

If your family member is struggling at school or work because of social or emotional issues, such as bullying or issues with their boyfriend or girlfriend, consider a therapist for your family member that specializes in working with that particular issue or age group. Sometimes people turn to drugs and alcohol to self-medicate when they feel like they don't fit it or are being bullied, and a good therapist can help sort this out.

Real-world situation: Your teen plays the "I don't care" card

In cases where the addict is a teen, I've had clients tell me, "My kid says he doesn't care if we take away his phone and the internet."

Don't get caught up in playing a game of escalation. When you are arguing with an active addict, who do you think is winning the argument? Not you. The most important thing you can do for your loved one is to show you love them by setting good boundaries and teaching them how to be responsible and accountable. Avoid arguing, shaming, bullying, threatening or raising your voice, but stick to a matter-of-fact conversation.

As working professionals, the best managers in our lives are likely those who communicated very clear expectations, timelines and policies. These managers are supportive and want you to succeed, and if you're struggling with completing work quickly and efficiently, these managers will offer support to alleviate the situation.

This is exactly the kind of supportive family member you want to be – like the best manager you ever had. Make your expectations clear and concise, always be available for support and advice, and remember that your job is to administer consequences and rewards.

Real-world situation: It's convenient for *me* if my loved one has a phone

If your addicted family member is a teen, they may need a phone for your convenience as a parent, but they don't necessarily need a smartphone. Provide an old-fashioned flip-phone that doesn't have internet. Clients have told me this works like a charm, as few kids would want to take a flip-phone out of their pocket for their friends to see. Your service providers can also set restrictions, such as time restrictions for when the phone will and will not operate and contact restrictions. A phone can be programmed to only allow calls to you or emergency services.

Restrictions can be applied to your internet access. It takes some creativity, but you can control what devices access your Wi-Fi, change your Wi-Fi password, or turn off Wi-Fi altogether. But if your child has homework that requires internet access, watch them do their homework or restrict the Wi-Fi access to a timeframe.

Restricting access to phones and Wi-Fi also includes other technologies, such as an iPad, tablet or Xbox. Are you nervous that you won't win a battle over physically taking the phone from your loved one? Simply call your service provider to turn off the device and change the Wi-Fi password. Removing access to the internet and phone quickly and effectively gives your loved one a wake-up call. But the positive results and improvement in your loved one's behavior won't occur if you don't stick to these actions.

Real-world situation: Incentivizing good behavior (part two)

It's important to positively incentivize good behavior. These incentives can be renewed access to privileges, such as limited time with the kids, or in cases where the addict is your teen, their car, phone, technologies and social life.

Remember: drugs and alcohol are never an acceptable incentive. This is not a negotiation and getting high is never on the table as an incentive.

Timelines for Improvement

Give your family member 30 days to show progress: drug tests are coming back with lower numbers or are close to being clean, better performance, including grades and attendance at school or work, and positive behavior at home. Always reward improvement and effort by acknowledging your family member and their accomplishments.

Thirty days is enough time to show improvement from a person who is abusing alcohol and marijuana. But what if your family member is abusing stronger drugs such as cocaine, heroin, opiates, methamphetamine or MDMA and benzodiazepines? Don't wait 30 days as death can be immediate. Jump to a different plan, the topic of the next chapter.

KEY TAKEAWAYS:

- Hold your "No drugs or alcohol" boundary accountable with a drug test—either a urine test or hair follicle test and a breathalyzer or a SoberLink®.

- You set the rules.

- Set separate boundaries, accountability, and structure for behavior at home and behavior at school or work.

- If the addict in your family is your teen and he or she needs a phone for your convenience, get them a flip phone until they follow your boundaries.

- If your family member is abusing alcohol and/or marijuana, give them a 30-day window to clean up their act. And make sure you test them at least weekly.

- Remember, when you are arguing, you are not winning.

- It's critical that you lead by example. What's good for your family member is good for everyone.

WORKSHEET

WEEK 1

Circle the appropriate response for each boundary.

Boundary	Was it Met?	Notes
No drugs, no alcohol	Y / N	
Regular school or work attendance	Y / N	
Regular therapy attendance	Y / N	
No lying	Y / N	
No hitting	Y / N	
No shouting	Y / N	
No cheating	Y / N	
Chores got done in a timely fashion	Y / N	

WEEK 2

Circle the appropriate response for each boundary.

Boundary	Was it Met?	Notes
No drugs, no alcohol	Y / N	
Regular school or work attendance	Y / N	
Regular therapy attendance	Y / N	
No lying	Y / N	
No hitting	Y / N	
No shouting	Y / N	
No cheating	Y / N	
Chores got done in a timely fashion	Y / N	

WEEK3

Circle the appropriate response for each boundary.

Boundary	Was it Met?	Notes
No drugs, no alcohol	Y / N	
Regular school or work attendance	Y / N	
Regular therapy attendance	Y / N	
No lying	Y / N	
No hitting	Y / N	
No shouting	Y / N	
No cheating	Y / N	
Chores got done in a timely fashion	Y / N	

WEEK 4

Circle the appropriate response for each boundary.

Boundary	Was it Met?	Notes
No drugs, no alcohol	Y / N	
Regular school or work attendance	Y / N	
Regular therapy attendance	Y / N	
No lying	Y / N	
No hitting	Y / N	
No shouting	Y / N	
No cheating	Y / N	
Chores got done in a timely fashion	Y / N	

chapter five

PLAN B

Chapter 5

Plan B

You tried Plan A for 30 days, but your family member is still using drugs and alcohol, failing to meet your expectations at school or work, and not improving behavior at home. Or, you skipped Plan A and need a new course of action because your family member has become involved with harder drugs than alcohol or marijuana that can cause death after just one use, such as heroin or cocaine. If this is the case, you need to implement a more immediate solution.

Let's talk about what substance abuse treatment looks like and how to access it.

Your Options for Plan B

Here's an overview of what the continuum of care looks like for substance abuse treatment:

- Medical detox facility
  - Patients are monitored at all hours of the day and night by trained staff members to first get the drugs and alcohol out of their system and then medically stabilize them. This process can take anywhere from three to seven days, depending on the severity of the chemical dependency.
- Residential treatment center (RTC)
  - Commonly referred to as in-patient rehab, RTC programs start at a minimum of 21 days and can last up to 90 days, depending on the client, the severity of the case, and the insurance reimbursement. RTC is not only for substance abuse abatement, but also for establishing support groups, individual therapy, group therapy, and psychiatric care. Patients can meet other patients who are becoming clean and participate in intensive programs designed to help patients figure out what to do when they are sober and leave the facility. Patients will also

receive family therapy, experiential therapy, life skills sessions, and psycho-education on a daily and weekly basis.

- Partial hospitalization program, or a PHP
  - o Most patients complete an RTC and then go to the PHP level of care. These therapeutic programs tend to consist of at least 20 hours a week of programming and can include individual therapy, group therapy, psychiatric consultations, and life skills training classes. Highly therapeutic, PHPs intend to help the patient resolve the reasons he or she uses substances and help them work through it in a supportive environment. A PHP can last up to three months depending on the needs of the client. The goal of the PHP is to start the reintegration process from RTC back home. More often than not, PHP is done in conjunction with a sober living facility.

- Intensive outpatient program (IOP)
  - o These programs are at least ten hours a week with the same programming as a PHP, but usually allow the patient more time away from the program to get back to living at home, attending school, working if they have a job, and practicing the life skills they are hopefully learning from the program. IOPs still have a stringent set of rules and expect that the patient will not be late

or miss a single appointment. At some facilities, their ability to complete the program depends on the patient's attendance. An IOP can last for three months or longer depending on the needs of the client.

- Sober living home
  - A sober living facility is a group house that is run by a sober house manager. The sober living houses have strict house rules and administer regular drug tests, but do not offer therapeutic programming other than regular house meetings and possibly a few mandatory 12-step meetings. The primary reason for the lack of therapy is it is expected the patient will continue therapy and psychiatric consultation on their own time outside of the sober living house, or they're engaged in PHP or IOP already and want to live in a sober environment. Sober living houses allow the patient to reintegrate into his or her previous life before detoxification, while being surrounded and supported by others who are facing the same struggle. Sober living can last anywhere from three months to 12 months depending on the facility and the needs of the client.

It is recommended that six continuous months of treatment, 30 RTC and 15 days of extended care (PHP, IOP, OP and sober living), are needed to effectively reverse the effects drugs and alcohol have on the body and the mind, while 24 months is recommended for those who have developed a severe opiate or benzodiazepine addiction. All statistics show that the longer a person stays in the treatment continuum, the better their chances are of staying sober long term.

What's Next?

Now that you've decided implementing a more intense plan can resolve your family member's addiction, it's time to find an appropriate facility for them. No family ever comes to this decision lightly, and few consider this option until it's a life-or-death crisis. Admittedly, it is hard to be proactive and take your time searching through all of your treatment program options when you are terrified your child, spouse, parent, or sibling may die from an overdose. This scenario often leads people to make hasty decisions, and unfortunately, some treatment centers can implement shady business practices by preying upon families in this situation. But you can avoid this situation by understanding a few guidelines to consider when deciding to send your family member to an intensive rehab.

Special Considerations for Women

Holly Wilson, MA, LPCC, is the founder of Women's Recovery in Denver, Colorado. She's an expert in the benefits of gender-specific treatment for women and was recently the featured guest on Episode 8 of my Chronic Hope podcast, which you can watch or listen to on YouTube. She advises families dealing with addiction to ask someone in the industry for a program recommendation.

Holly is in recovery herself and went to a 60-day co-ed program. However, her Sober Living program was women only. It was self-governed, and Holly shared that the level women were able to open up to in the all-women environment was so much more profound and in-depth than in the co-ed environment. She explained there are several reasons women aren't seeking the treatment they need.

Here are some of the things Holly often hears as a leader in the field:

- "I can't leave my family." Wanting to keep the family unit intact is a major concern for women. Holly cites the following statistic: 90% of the time when a man goes into treatment, the wife will stay; 10% of the time when a woman goes into treatment, the husband will stay.

She recently had a client say she had to ask her husband to babysit his own children so she could get treatment!

- "I can't leave my job; I don't know if it'll be there when I get back." Women are paid less than men, and often valued less than men in the workplace. Taking time off the career or job path for treatment can come with higher risks.

- "It's not that bad." Women have learned over time how to show up and look pretty. They can more easily hide hangovers. Also, women tend to have a higher pain threshold than men and experience more pressure from those around them to "handle things." Unfortunately, the telescoping effect means substances wreak havoc on women's bodies worse than men even if you can't see it from the outside. Women have health consequences from substance abuse faster than men do as their body composition is different.

- Women are less likely to be put into homelessness than men.

- For women with trauma, the presence of men can be a real challenge to healing. They feel reluctant to feel vulnerable in front of men. Trauma is uncovered in layers; your body unlocks it over time and women need space and grace to move through it. Women who have a history of substance abuse often have traumas associated with it because when you're passed out somewhere dangerous as a woman, you are very vulnerable.

Holly's program offers IOP as an entry level of care and started growing quickly. By using this approach, they ultimately ended up getting more women into in-patient treatment after building rapport. Once patients trusted Holly's team, they were then willing to take the recommendation to go to a higher level of care. However, childcare is a challenge for mothers; Women's Recovery asks for 10-12 hours per week from clients to start.

Ultimately, in a male dominated society, there is a difference in how men and women move through recovery. There is a pressure on women to appear "nice" which can get in the way of being honest. They are more inclined to censor themselves in front of men. At Women's Recovery, Holly makes it a point not to have a dress code for anyone, not even her staff, saying, "We don't have to look cute here. We want to ugly cry."

The idea is to dispense with the whole concept of cute and ugly and just be. This whole concept of helping women find the gender-specific treatment they need is very important to me. When I was two years sober,

I started dating a woman in AA. My sponsor told me—rightly so—that women tend to come to recovery with stuff that men don't even understand. He said, "You are a big dude. When you were to pass out or be in dangerous situations, the odds of anything happening to you were minimal. But for women, it's different."

Selecting a Facility

Be honest about what you can afford. An RTC can cost $1,000 a day or more before insurance reimbursement and may not always be in-network with your insurance company. Be careful about a facility or program that says, "We take all insurance!" What that means is they will *bill* every insurance company. It doesn't mean that they are in your insurance company's network or that your insurance will cover their program.

While it may be tempting to Google "adolescent or teen treatment centers," you may likely find a list of places that have spent a lot of money on SEO and Google advertisements and may not actually be the best option. It's much better to turn to a word-of-mouth recommendation from someone familiar with the recovery community.

Beware of the people who leave a negative review of an RTC online. Most likely they are the patients who hated being there and have not completed the program or did not stay sober. Contact the RTC directly and ask if you can speak with some families that they have worked with. I have found that these families will be very candid with you about their experiences. Also, you can ask your family therapist if they know of any addiction therapists in your town or if they have a list of in-state and out-of-state facilities. If you can't find answers to those questions, I have provided resources at the end of this chapter where you can find the appropriate treatment programs.

There are services that work with families to help them in this process. Educational consultants, treatment consultants, interventionists, family case managers and recovery coaches are some of the roles you may come in contact with during your search. All of them can provide excellent guidance for a family searching for the right treatment program for their loved one. It's important to screen these people to make sure that you are not being taken advantage of in a time of crisis.

Consultants and Interventionists

Educational consultants specialize in working with families to help them determine their best treatment option. But there's a catch: these folks are expensive. Many consultants start at around $5,000. Good educational consultants will case manage the family and the addicted person, help the family find the right treatment center for their loved one, and then act as a liaison while the addicted person is in treatment. If your loved one needs extended care or a therapeutic boarding school, the consultant should be able to provide recommendations. Consultants typically have a relationship with each treatment center, extended care facility and therapeutic boarding school, and have personally visited each facility to meet with the staff, review the grounds and determine if it's a right fit for their clients.

Educational consultants are incredible people who do fantastic work, but not every family can afford to hire one. If you do choose to hire an educational consultant, always ask the consultant if they are getting a commission from any of the places they are recommending. If they are, that may skew their recommendation and may not be the best choice for your family member's treatment. It is critical to know if you are being steered into a facility for financial compensation, so ask ahead of time to ensure that this is not the case.

A good interventionist is worth their weight in gold. They can help guide the family through the process of finding an appropriate treatment program and having the hard discussion with their family member about going to treatment. And they can help the family make the plan for how to confront their loved one and offer help (the actual intervention). Most addiction therapists, psychiatrists, and treatment programs will have an interventionist that they have worked with and can recommend. The cost can range from free to $25,000 depending on the level of services provided. Remember that everything is negotiable. Finally, be sure to ask for references and call them!

I recently spoke to Charles (Charlie) Van Leuven NCRC ll, NCLAMA, the Owner-Operator of National Treatment Transport, an expert interventionist I greatly respect. He had some insights to share about the job of the interventionist and what to expect when you hire one. The interventionist, Charlie explains, is a mediator who is going to plan out the intervention and then run it. He or she needs to have the ability to connect with all the family members and be really thorough, meaning it is important for that interventionist to interview every member of the family ahead of time. The goal is to find out if, for example, the addict's uncle was in a car crash with the addict two years ago and the addict blames him for his subsequent drug use. There is always someone you *don't* want at the intervention, but the person who hires the interventionist may not know who that person is.

You want an interventionist who knows what they are doing, and it's a job best handled in pairs, meaning it's a two-person team. The only thing that matters in an intervention is getting the addict to agree to go to treatment. That's it. It's not the interventionist's job to be sure everyone in the room is "heard." You want an interventionist who has a plan. Do they have flights booked? Do they have a car? The interventionist can't wing any of it.

Once the person says yes, they will go to treatment, their willingness is fleeting. The second you get them to say yes, they should be packing a bag and then headed *out the door*. With adolescent intervention, at the end of the day, they don't have a choice and they have to go, but about five to seven percent of the time, they'll try to run off. Thus, Charlie's whole staff consists of big guys, but the goal is to de-escalate the situation. "We really just get them to a point where we can reason with them," he said. "Sometimes kids want to run away and we stop them by saying something like, 'Hey man, you don't have a choice. What we know is how you act right now determines how long you'll be in treatment. We are all trying to figure out how much help you need. If you fight it, you'll be in treatment FOREVER. You're never going to see your friends. But if you participate, you'll be home in no time. We'll have them do breathing exercises if they're hyperventilating, but it doesn't happen that often. Once we show up, they know it's real."

I also asked Charlie, "What do you wish more families understood about what you do?" and he said, "Families need to understand that just because it's cheap, doesn't mean it's a good deal. There are some things you don't want a discount on."

The average price of an adult interventionist is $5k. For an adolescent, it's $3,500 for a long-distance transport (this is for up to 24 hours of care). Someone who is going to take custody of your child? You get what you pay for. Ask, does this person have insurance? Do they have a plan? What is the plan? Charlie told a quick story about one family who used a discount $1000 interventionist recently. The addict in that situation stole a car, started a high-speed chase, and ended up in a psych ward for two weeks. That interventionist made some serious mistakes.

"I am there to get them the help they need," Charlie said. If they accept the help, great. It's not about anybody else. It's about saving this person's life."

Charlie sticks to three simple talking points when he conducts an intervention:

- **What do we see?** "You're killing yourself; you've lost your job." We are presenting the facts. "We know what's going on. We love you. We are here in a very vulnerable capacity because we care about you. We are willing to let you be pissed at us because we care about you." According to an old school AA quote, "If a drug addict is happy, you're hurting them." If you're doing what they want, you're a problem. Because what they want is killing them. This includes money, shelter, and even emotional support.

- **What do we fear?** "This is going to go on, you're going to overdose and die."

- **What do we hope?** "That you'll stop using and turn your life around."

Love in Action

I want to give you an additional perspective on how interventions work. Keith Bradley, the founder of Love in Action Interventions and Training in Greeley, Colorado, is a friend and colleague of mine whose approach I greatly respect. I refer dozens of families to him and we speak to each other a daily basis. I am including Keith's input here on both his process and his advice for families who are considering reading out to an interventionist. "Certification, liability insurance, and references are three important factors in selecting an interventionist," Keith began when I asked him to give us an overview of his work. "It's very significant that the interventionist be certified because it allows that professional to buy liability insurance."

References can be a bit tricky due to the private nature of what an interventionist does. "When I talk to somebody who needs a reference," Keith explained, "I need to respect of the privacy of the families I've worked with previously. So, I say, 'Here are three different treatment centers I've been working with for 10 years. They know what my work is about and if it's not good, they're not going to recommend me.' I don't ever ask a client's family to give me a recommendation."

Next, length of time in business is important, as in how experienced is the interventionist? In Keith's case, the answer is 14 years. "I've done 606 interventions myself and I do a much better job today than I did 10 years ago as a result of being able to draw on that experience," he said. "It makes you sharper over time. You only have to make one mistake one time with an intervention. If you're serious about what you're doing, you'll never make the same mistake again. We are dealing with life and death situations. A lot of times, it's not only alcohol and drug related intervention; it's crisis intervention.

"I believe the initial call is the most significant part of the entire process, because the person on the other end is very likely to be in the darkest hour they've ever experienced," Keith said. "In other words, I'm not getting the call where they say, 'Hey, I think my kid might have smoked a joint at lunch in high school today.' I'm getting, 'My husband's been to treatment several different times yet refuses to acknowledge that he even needs help right now. We don't know what to do.'"

Keith has a process, a format for the interventions he runs, which is rather unique. The reality show *Intervention* is not real, he explained; it's all based on past cases. But it put the idea of holding an intervention in the media and made people aware of this process who would have never been aware otherwise. So, the upside of that show is more people are interested in knowing what it is that interventionists do and how they accomplish their goal. However, the show uses an ultimatum-based format. Keith does not: "I use a very loving process from a spiritual perspective. I don't know how anyone could do it under any other circumstances because the process I use is very valuable. It's not an experiment. I know what works the highest percentage of the time.

"We're offering the addicted person—the AP—a gift of love. To a large degree, the people that we're intervening on are overwhelmed with the fact that their family loves them so much. That they're not jumping ship. This is important because the disease of alcoholism and drug addiction creates a lot of shame. The individual doesn't feel worthy of the love from their family; they feel like they've destroyed it. As part of the process I've developed, the family members write these very heartfelt letters, and we read the letters at the intervention. It brings the walls of denial down."

Careful Prior Planning and Lived Experience

"With the model that I use, if they're going out of state, we buy airline tickets in advance to take them from the intervention to treatment," Keith said. "Between 75% to 80% of the time, we go from the intervention straight to the treatment center. It's a very high success rate."

He points to his personal experience with addiction as significant: "I'm not saying you have to be in recovery yourself to do what I do, but when I'm leading an intervention, I'm speaking from my own experience. Sometimes, that's the most valuable asset I have: when I can look at an individual and say, 'I know what it's like to go through withdrawal from opiates. I know what it's like to wake up in the morning and have to drink three ounces of vodka in order to shave.' The most negative aspect of my entire life is, today, one of my biggest assets because they're not talking to somebody who has 14 initials behind their name. They're talking to somebody who has actually walked in their shoes, and been successful getting clean and sober and *remaining* clean and sober."

While Keith and his small team don't use an ultimatum-based process, they do believe in boundaries. As a general rule, between 30 and 40 hours goes into counseling and training the family members for an event that generally takes a little over two hours. This is done so everyone is on the same page ahead of the event. Keith knows in advance, in most cases, what the AP's primary objection for going to treatment is going to be. He prepares in advance how they are going to answer that objection during the intervention. They have a plan. It's basically the same as what an attorney does, he said. An attorney figures out what the objections are going to be and how he or she is going to overcome them.

There's a lot that goes into it, down to the arrangement of who is going to sit where in the intervention itself. For example, if there's somebody that your loved one is always mad at, Keith won't put that person directly across from them in the room. He can't allow it to become a debate. Instead, he helps to bring the truth to the table through the letters that are read.

Spiritual Fitness

"We've got a proven process that works very well," Keith explained. "The interaction starts with the initial phone call. And for me to be effective with what I do, I personally have to be spiritually fit. Every day, on awakening, I meditate and pray, to make the connection with the higher presence. You can call it whatever you want, but I have to get spiritually connected every day in my life as there's no canned speech that I use when I'm talking to a family. Yet because of my spiritual fitness, I'm always given the words. What I do to stay clean and sober *allows* me to do the work and I think the spiritual component is one of the biggest differences in the format that I use. That's just the path that I've been on; I pray and meditate every day because I never know when my phone rings, who's going to be there or what kind of crisis is actually going on. If I'm spiritually fit, I'm not standing in judgment of what's going on. If I'm spiritually fit, I am a good listener. I become all the things that I need to be in order to be effective. The job that I do is not for everybody. It's a lot of work and it's very time consuming. It's a commitment. I can't tell you the number of Thanksgivings and Christmases in which I've thrown my fork in the plate and said, 'I have to take this call.' The work is very time sensitive.

"After the initial phone call, the first thing that we do is figure out what's going to be the appropriate treatment center for that specific individual—whether there are funds in place to pay for treatment, or if they're insurance dependent. I always give families a minimum of two choices in terms of treatment facilities. These are people that I've had long-term relationships with—a good track record. Once we decide the direction we're going to go in, the next thing I do is reach out to all prospective members of the team, and set up a conference call. Everybody that's going to participate in the intervention has to be on that call. I do this to have the opportunity to address them individually about what effect this person's addiction has had on them. I help them make certain that in writing their letters, they only include first-hand information. I want to know how your family member's substance use affected *you*. We would never start a statement in the letters with, 'Well, mom says…' It has to do with *your* personal interaction with your loved one, how *you've* been affected.

"To give you an example of the flow of the letters, I'll use a mother's perspective. It might begin with something like, 'The best day of my life was the day you were born.' It'll include all of the things they loved about watching their son or daughter grow up and who they became through grade school, middle school, and high school. Maybe they were an athlete or maybe they were an academic standout or whatever was. Then, we get into what's happened since the drug abuse began, to the point of it affecting every area of that person's life. It's all about the truth. We want the letters to end up saying, 'I want my son back.' Or, 'I want my daughter back.' Or, 'Sister, I feel like I've lost you and I want you back.'

"It's very heartfelt and it's very, *very* emotional. I generally arrive the day before the intervention. I try to get as early a flight as I can. We do a family meeting practice rehearsal the day before the intervention itself. That's where we talk about the arrangement of the chairs. We talk about the order in which each person is going to read their letters. I want the most emotional person in the room to be the first one to read their letter. I want to get the emotion going as early as I can.

"We pack a bag in advance if at all possible. All of that is in place. When I first meet the individual, I don't have a canned speech but it's something along the lines of, 'I've been talking to your family now for two or three weeks and we want to offer you a solution to everything you've got going on.' As long as I can keep it solution-based, it doesn't become an attack. It doesn't become an ambush. It's a very, very loving process. I say something like, 'The only deception that's involved in what we're talking about today was me showing up unannounced. There'll be no more than deception beyond that.' We know exactly who's going to read their letters first, so when I feel like I'm getting the crossed arms and body language that says *I'm not hearing a thing you're saying*, then I say, 'Why don't you start?'

"I can't overstate how well we have to prepare, prior to the intervention, to get the outcome we're looking for. You have to be able to think out of the box. I've done hundreds of interventions, and they all have some similarities but no two were alike. Fortunately, the family is going to tell you if they think their loved one is going to be a runner in advance. The entire team doesn't go chasing after him; the person that has the best connection with the individual and myself go and retrieve him. As a matter of fact, that happens 35% of the time: they do walk out. Of that 35%, we've been able to retrieve above 70% of them. I say, 'There's no way I can make you do anything.' We have to get him or her into the idea that they need to do this."

Transports

"I do 99% of all my own transports. When I'm transporting that person to a treatment center, it never ceases to amaze me the things they will share with someone they just met four hours ago—that they wouldn't consider sharing with a family member. It comes back to the bond that's created because they know I walked in their shoes. It allows there to be connection. When I'm delivering the person that I intervened on, within the next 24 hours, I do an assessment of them based on the time we spent together. I give the treatment center information right up front; I do it with every case. This is vital information for them to have. I'm giving them details it might otherwise take 14 days to extract. I hand it to them on a platter: the dynamic of the family, all that stuff. Yet a lot of interventions don't transport their own clients. I think it's one of the most significant parts of the intervention.

"We're not God's gift to the intervention world, but we really do good work. When my phone rings, and a family commits to doing an intervention, we're only going to get one shot," Keith concluded. "We have to make the most of it. I've been doing this for a while now and it's the most rewarding thing that I've ever done...and I don't mean financially. I turned 68 years old this month and I'm still chasing athletes over rooftops. It's the most emotional thing that I've ever done. It's the most stressful thing. Hence the need to be spiritually fit."

Family Case Management

Aside from education consultants and interventionists, there are firms and agencies that specialize in family case management. These companies have relationships with treatment centers across the country, and offer help with sober transportation, interventions, case management, choosing a treatment center and working with the family before, during, and after the addict goes to treatment.

Family case management is a relatively new concept and comes with mixed reviews. Good case management comes with weekly contact with the family and the addict and can include planning for the intervention, working with the family while the addict is in treatment and helping the family plan for reintegration when treatment is over. A good case manager will have suggestions of resources for the family for therapy, support groups, and reading materials to help them understand addiction and how it affects the family.

Yes, there are predators out there waiting for families in crisis to jump on the first "nice-sounding" solution and accept giving any amount of money to keep their family member alive. While the recovery business is very much a word-of-mouth reputation industry, it's critical that families spend some time proactively looking for resources and avoiding hasty decisions. Ask everyone you talk to for references from other families that they have worked with and don't be shy about asking questions. This is your family member's life we are talking about and it's critical that you are direct and don't hold back when interviewing.

The quality of the therapy and the staff is important to note when you're looking into a facility. It's who they're hiring, and their skill sets. Unfortunately, every state has its own terminology, its own set of rules, and its own requirements. That's why word of mouth is so important—reputation is everything in this industry. Red flags to watch out for: are the inmates are running the asylum? Is it organized? Is it on target? Does it have a family program? Do they engage the family in the treatment process? Do they have licensed therapists? Do they have a doctor or nurse on staff?

Leverage and Unity

The whole point of the Plan B intervention is saying, "Hey, we love you. But if you don't go to treatment for your addiction, you don't get to see the kids, you don't get to be part of a family, and you're moving out today." The point is to present a united front for the addict. It's not just the spouse. It's also their parents, siblings, co-workers. You're all on the same page. So, if the addict chooses not to go to treatment, they're choosing not to be part of the family; they're putting their career at risk.

Because the stakes are high, that's where the coaching of the family becomes so significant. An interventionist works to keep that family cohesive and not breaking apart. Interventionists are kind of like the ER doctor. They come in, they deal with a crisis, and they move on. Some actually deliver the person to the treatment program; they coordinate with the family ahead of time.

A question that the family is always asking me is: "Why does the intervention have to be a secret? Why does it have to be a surprise? Why does it have to be a confrontation?" And the answer is *it's the only way that works.* When you try to bring someone who's high in on the conversation about what to do, no progress will be made whatsoever. If you say, "Hey, we're going to meet with interventionists," your addicted family member will go into full overdrive to avoid having to make a change. They start dividing up the family, as in, "I can't believe you're doing this, you never loved me." It fractures the family. The way things get screwed up is families cave.

The addict will say things like, "I'll go, but I'm only going to outpatient."

No.

Or, "I'll go, but I'm going across the street."

No.

Or, "I'll go, but I'm picking the place."

No.

The point is, they think they're going to angle their way through this and do what they want to do. But that's not going to happen. Your addicted family member is no longer in charge.

"These are the rules now. And we love you."

Set up Interviews

You have your lists of in-state options, out-of-state options, in-network facilities, and out-of-network facilities. Or, you've obtained a list of options from your therapist, consultant, or case manager. Now it's time to set up phone interviews or visit each facility or center in-person if you have the time. When speaking to the marketing representative at each RTC, request to speak with the clinical director, if possible. The clinical director should be able to tell you what the overall philosophy of the facility is and how they go about achieving success with their patients. They will also be able to tell you who they have the most success with, remember not all treatment centers are the same just as not all patients are the same.

This process of due diligence is about making sure you are finding the best fit. Ask the facility representative if they have a list of families who have used the facility in the past and are willing to share their experiences with you. It is also wise to ask the representative what issues families struggle with at their facility. Note that if the representative cannot answer that question honestly and directly, you should not be interested in that facility. You want a facility that caters to specific problems and issues.

Don't be shy about asking the facility representative if the facility has faced any issues in the past, such as legal problems. If they have given you a list of clients, ask the clients the same question. No facility is perfect, but it is important that you send your family member to a place that will care for them and help them through fighting their addiction.

Additional questions you should ask:

- How long has the program been in business?
- Does the program hold accreditation with CARF, or the Joint Commission, and are they certified by LegitScript?

- Is the program licensed by the state to treat substance use disorders and mental health?

- Are there full-time, board certified doctors on staff? How frequently can patients meet with doctors?

- Do the therapists have a master's degree or licenses? Do they have specialized substance use disorder (SUD) training?

- Does the program use data-informed, evidenced-based therapies?

- Does the program incorporate family therapy in the treatment process?

- Is there a family program that you can attend while your family member is in treatment?

- Are treatment plans individualized for your family member's specific needs?

- Does the program offer dual diagnosis treatment? Can the program treat someone who struggles with addiction and a concurrent mental health condition? How do they accomplish this?

- Where do individuals live while in treatment and what level of supervision do they receive?

- How many individuals share a room?

- How long is the wait to get into treatment?

- Are the detoxification medications FDA approved?

- Can I use insurance to cover the cost of treatment? In network or out of network benefits?

- What kind of support is offered after completing the program?

Doing your due diligence is critical in this step. Do not make a hasty decision out of panic or fatigue. Ask your trusted friends what they think. Meet others who are going through the same thing, and understand that you are not the only family to be dealing with this situation. Find out if it is possible for you to meet with other families who have had family members in the facility that you are considering, and listen to their experiences. Trust your instincts: if you think you are being hustled by a sweet-talking business development representative from a treatment center that has all the answers, then you probably are.

Ask your therapist for their input, and see if they know anyone else who would be willing to share their experiences with the facilities you are considering. This will require some paperwork and time, but it is worth it. And while you are doing all of this, try to avoid falling into the shame spiral of thinking: *What did we do wrong to make our family member use drugs and need treatment?* There will be plenty of time for that after your family member is in treatment and while you continue with family therapy and your own individual therapy, but right now, focus on getting your family member the help needed as quickly as possible.

Don't be shy about talking finances with the treatment programs—they are all businesses that survive on referrals, and they need you just as much as you need them.

Everything is negotiable. Be open and honest with representatives about your situation. Some facilities have scholarship programs and financing options. Many times, you can find ways to work with the facility.

Visit the Facility

If you have the time and funds to travel, it's a wise decision to visit the facility in advance and investigate the place. When visiting the facility, ask if you can see their programming for the week, the rooms patients stay, eat a meal and see what the dining facility looks like, and meet some of the staff members. Additional questions you can ask:

- Do you have an exercise facility, equine therapy, art therapy, play therapy or trauma therapy?
- If so, then what kind is it? Can I talk to the therapists who will be providing these therapies?
- What is the philosophy of the clinical team?

- How did your team arrive at that perspective? Why?

- What is the expectation for family involvement? Is there a family program and weekly phone calls or therapy?

Note there is a list of questions in the back of this book for you to take with you as a guide.

Some facilities offer wilderness programs. These are therapeutic treatment programs that offer 30, 60 and 90-day outdoor experiential programs where patients are required to learn how to take care of themselves, be part of a team, and be responsible to the group. These programs are very effective in helping particularly young people mature, build self-confidence, and improve self-esteem. And the program connects children to one another and to the experience they are going through, without any of the distractions of the modern world. My clients and their kids have had wonderful experiences with wilderness programs, so it is worth considering this option if the addicted person in your family is a minor.

Nikki Soda is the Membership Development Officer of the National Association of Addiction Treatment Providers (NAATP). I respect her expertise on the topic of how to choose the best treatment center for your family member's specific needs. Here are the key points she advises you consider while evaluating treatment options:

1. Ensure the facility is **licensed** by the state and **accredited** by an entity like Joint Commission or CARF, the Commission on Accreditation of Rehabilitation Facilities. This is important, because it means that they are following guidelines and have appropriate and regular oversight.

2. Ask who serves as medical director. **Look at the staff.** Are they all licensed? Make sure they have a staff page on their website. It's a prerequisite in order to be a member of the NAATP.

3. Look at the **longevity** of the program. How long have they been around? What's their history? I'm more inclined to send someone to a place that's been around a long time.

4. Look at **outcomes**. The majority of treatment centers have an outcomes tool. Patients are followed up with upon discharge. Frequently at the beginning, then it lessens over time. Specific questions are answered. Outcomes are often available to the public to see. Outcomes should be on the list.

5. Know the **diagnosis** of the addicted person and find a treatment center that specializes in that diagnosis. Is it primary Substance Use

Disorder (SUD) with a secondary Mental Health diagnosis? Or primary Mental Health with secondary SUD? The behaviors of the addicted person are a big deal. Sometimes it's important to look for a behaviorally-focused program, like a wilderness program. But that may not be a good idea at all if there are mental health issues.

6. For adolescents, ask what type of **education resources** they have at their facility. Can it integrate school into treatment if appropriate? Is there an Educational Director?

"Marketing can be so deceptive," Nikki cautions. "Have a discussion with the clinical director, not the marketer. Get the schedule, the real nuts and bolts of what happens each day inside the facility. Find out what family involvement looks like."

She gives the following links to check out for additional helpful information here:

- hazeldenbettyford.org/treatment/choosing-addiction-treatment-center
- addictionpolicy.org/post/navigating-treatment-and-addiction-a-guide-for-families

Getting your family member to treatment

You've figured out your budget and your program, now the question becomes, how will you get your family member to the treatment facility? If they are willing to go, then you're in luck. This does actually happen and it makes the transition to the treatment center much smoother. Sometimes individuals are aware of their substance abuse and actually welcome the opportunity to seek help. These individuals will pack up their stuff and get in the car, knowing their life needs to change.

But what if your family member is not so thrilled with the idea of treatment or an extended wilderness experience? Talk to the treatment center about a sober transportation service, as this is how most individuals get to treatment.

If you choose this option, know what to expect. Two people will come to your house and meet with you ahead of time. They will organize when and where they are going to pick up your family member. Generally, this is done early in the morning at your house, and it should happen very quickly and efficiently. The sober escorts arrive at the assigned time, wake up your family member, and let them know what's happening. They will give them a choice to pack a bag, or the escorts will pack one for them. After the bag is packed, your family member will have a chance to say goodbyes. The sober escorts then either drive them to the airport or directly to the treatment program. This is always a hard experience for families. But remember: you are at the point of wanting to intervene with someone who is literally killing themselves with drugs and alcohol.

Although it may be hard to say goodbye to your family member and send them off to a treatment center, it is the only thing that you have left that you can do. It is important to choose the right facility and to know what to expect while your family member is in treatment. You will need to know what things will look like when they get out, and what they will have to do to continue on their new sober path. Letting go of them in order to allow them to receive help can be difficult. But it is necessary.

Plan C

You may be asking, "What if my family member is over 18? What if my addict is my spouse or my sibling or my parent?" I have used Plan A and Plan B with adults and I add Plan C. Plan C is if the addict is unwilling to follow boundaries, accountability, and consequences (Plan A), and they refuse to go to the treatment program or facility you've chosen (Plan B), then the family, spouse, or siblings can let the adult addict know that until the substance abuse stops and the behavior changes, the addict is no longer welcome as part of the family. This is exactly what happened to me in 1991.

My family got help from some professionals that told them to set boundaries with me and let me know that in no uncertain terms, until I quit drinking and using drugs, I was not welcome as part of the family anymore. It is critical that the whole family is in agreement before taking this tact. I recommend working with a therapist, a family case manager or an interventionist and making a plan and holding your line.

My favorite statement to share with families is, "We love you too much to keep watching you kill yourself." It's compassionate. One response I get from families where the adult addict is still living with them is: "If we kick them out, they will go live on the streets and kill themselves!"

My response is direct, "They are already killing themselves and you're facilitating it by allowing it to happen in your home. Why not offer them an alternative?" If the addict chooses to leave the home because they don't want to get sober, then tell them you love them and will respect their choices but they cannot continue to live at home and use. Every time they call or text, you should respond with the same message, "We love you and want you to get help. Are you ready to quit using?"

The alternative is to allow the addict to keep dying a slow death in the home and have that effect the entire family. This is not the old "tough love" approach of locking them out and turning your back on them. This approach is about telling the addict that you love them and will do anything to help them get help if they are ready. But until they are ready, you need to set a firm boundary. It has been my experience, personally and professionally, that this is the approach that works. Sometimes, however, it takes weeks or months for the addict to test the boundaries and eventually see that the family means business.

KEY TAKEAWAYS:

- The continuum of care starts with detox, RTC, PHP, IOP and sober living homes. Choose the one that's right for you and your family member. Note that the addicted person doesn't get to select where they go.

- Your family therapist may be the best resource for choosing a treatment option.

- Don't be afraid to ask to speak with other families that have been through this process before you.

- Do your research before picking a treatment facility and don't be afraid to ask questions.

- You can engage an educational consultant, interventionist, or a family case manager in the process of picking treatment options. Make sure you ask them for references.

- If you have the time, try to visit some of the programs that you are considering.

- If the addict is an adult, you can still use Plan C if they refuse Plans A and B.

- Plan for 90 days to six months of treatment at a minimum. Seventy-five to 80% of addicts do 30-day programs only, without follow-up care, and then go back and relapse

WORKSHEET

How to pick an interventionist:

These steps come from expert Charles Van Leuven NCRC II, NCLAMA, the Owner-Operator of National Treatment Transport, and Keith Bradley.

1. **Step one:** Ask for a word-of-mouth referral for an interventionist from a professional in the recovery community, such as your family therapist.

2. **Step two:** Understand you get what you pay for, and the average fee for a skilled interventionist is $5,000. Be sure your interventionist is insured.

3. **Step three:** Ask for the interventionist's plan of action. The plan should include detailed travel arrangements.

4. **Step four:** Ask for at least three recent references (other families this individual has worked with in the last month).

5. **Step five:** Keep in mind that the best interventionists often work in teams of two.

How to choose a treatment facility

1. The first question is always, **"Cash or insurance?"** You'll engage with someone like me or an interventionist who knows which facilities are in your insurance network. Those facilities will run your actual insurance card and tell you what the cost will be, say $5,000 for 30 days of treatment. This information will help you narrow down your list of options.

    Cash or Insurance? ....

2. The next step is to take stock of what's going on and any **special considerations**. If the addict is a woman who has a history of trauma, for example, the facility you choose should have sensitivity to that. And you'd probably want an all-female facility. Treatment centers are never one size-fits all

   Special considerations: _____

3. Then, decide if you want an **in-state or out-of-state** facility. I think out-of-state is better, frankly, because the family is often a huge part of the problem.

   In-state or out-of-state: _____

4. After the 30 days, there is PHP, partial hospitalization, which is 20 hours per week of care. Next, IOP (intensive outpatient) is 12 hours a week of the same thing. The last step is traditional outpatient therapy (that's me). All of this is under the umbrella of sober living. The idea is that we need to **slowly release the addict back into the wild.** 75 to 80% of addicts do 30 days only and then go back and relapse.

   Do you have a plan for six months of treatment?

   ....

5. If your family has the financial resources, consider the **90-day inpatient model**, as it is showing the best results. It's containing someone, and really working on stuff that's going on inside them, the hard part: the craving and the mental obsession. The continuous thought that "I'm not the problem, everyone else is the problem."

   Have you explored the 90-day in-patient model?

   ....

Part Two

During Treatment

1. Weekly meetings to discuss feelings and ask questions.

2. Seek family support groups and resources.

3. Understand and assess family dynamics.

chapter six

YOUR FAMILY MEMBER IS IN A TREATMENT FACILITY: NOW, TAKE A BREATH

Chapter 6

Your Family Member Is in a Treatment Facility: Now, Take a Breath

A question my clients often ask is, "My family member is in treatment, so what do I do now?" One of the saddest, yet common things about this process is that once an individual is in treatment, the family becomes invisible until the week before their loved one comes home. Acting this way is as if you're dropping off a family member at Best Buy, telling the salesperson they are broken, and explaining you will be back in 60 days to pick up the replacement.

The addict is in treatment, the problem is solved, so all is good, right?

Wrong.

You cannot expect your loved one to do something that you—and the entire family—is not willing to do as well. When an addict begins treatment and recovery, the family must follow. Note that your family will not necessarily have to *go* to treatment, but there are treatment centers that specialize in working through codependency and family of origin trauma alongside addiction. These may be noteworthy options for a family with multiple issues that need to be addressed.

Beginning to Address Codependency

Codependency is a common concurrent theme in families with addiction, and it easily becomes an issue for all family members. When parents become codependent in handling the kid with an addiction, for example, it is often detrimental to the other siblings or family members in the house, causing significant problems and trauma for everyone involved. In these instances, the addicted member becomes the focus of the family. This masks deeper issues within the family or marriage. Getting an addict to treatment is just the first step in healing the family; there's a larger recovery process for the whole system that must take place.

There was a lot of codependency in my own family of origin. My dad, my sister, and myself acted as if my mom's substance use was not wrong. It was normal. It was normal that we showed up two to three hours late to holidays and family events. It was normal to come home and find my mom in bed at lunchtime. It was normal for me to go to all my dad's events with him. But of course, none of that was normal. And us insisting so was simply a sign of codependency.

The ultimate example of this dynamic in my family was when my grandmother died, my dad's mom. We got a call at two or three in the morning, and we all gathered around my dad. He said, "They say we've got to get there now." My mom said, "Kevin will take you." So, I went to throw on some clothes. My sister was downstairs waiting for me. She saw I was frustrated that Mom wouldn't step up and said, "I know. I know, but Dad needs you." So, my dad and I went down there and said goodbye. I held my grandmother's hand while she died. Then, about half an hour later, my mom showed up. To me, this behavior revealed she was completely incapable of being there emotionally or taking care of herself on any level whatsoever. In the void she left, taking care of Dad became our responsibility.

In my family, Christmas was always this unhealthy game of, "Tell me what you want. Then, I'm going to get you something different and call you ungrateful." One year, my dad asked me to pick out a suitcase from a catalogue, which I did. I was traveling a lot for work and knew what I needed. But he gave the one I chose to my brother-in-law. I said, "I can't believe you." He responded by handing me another suitcase and said "I got you this one instead, I think it's better suited than the one that you picked out." It launched this huge battle; my mom took off. She just got in the car and bolted, even thought it was Christmas morning and we were expecting 25 people in three hours' time. My sister and I, without batting an eye, got to work cooking, cleaning up our mess, and trying to make everything alright. My brother-in-law was mystified; I was like, "This is our life!"

It was all damage control, all the time. I share these personal stories with you now to show I understand what you may be going through—and to explain how essential it is that the entire family work to change while an addict works to change. It's not one person's job—it's everyone's job.

The Family Ecosystem

When your family member is safe in a treatment facility, it is now time for you to take a breath. Again, this time period provides the opportunity to look at the larger family ecosystem. Ideally, families will engage in family therapy and individual therapy at least once every week. And it is always wise to attend therapy sessions at the treatment center if possible, so the family and treatment specialists can together create a plan for when your family member returns home. Rarely do people who go to treatment come from families that don't have some larger issues in tandem with the addiction.

The 30 to 90 days an addict is away in treatment is the best time for the family to start their own healing process, as it is easier to analyze what happened that could have contributed to the family member's addiction during this time. Work out solutions and restructure the family environment while the addict is safe and away at a treatment facility. Stop blaming each other for what went wrong, work together on repairing the family dynamic, and open up about individual issues.

I have often met with family members of addicts who tell me, "There is no addiction or mental health issues in our family *other than this one person.* No generational issues either. We have no idea how this happened!"

While I used to believe these families were lying to me to cover up some deep, dark secrets, in reality, many families don't actually *see* their own larger issues. Let's be honest. No one wants to admit that they have addictions or mental health issues because society shames, ostracizes, or simply views people differently once they have the courage to open up. But every family has something: I have never met a family that doesn't have something in the family tree that needs to be addressed. Despite this, I often hear "I am not the one with the problem, why do I have to go to therapy?" The answer? Addiction is a family disease. And it affects everyone who is engaged with the addict. Recovery takes the whole family.

Participating in recovery as an entire family is going to show you something crucial: that you're now out of the addict management business. There are two kinds of business: my business and not my business. The worst thing we can do is bring the addict home to a family system that hasn't changed. The family members of addicts often think that taking care of themselves is selfish, but it's really the opposite. You must, as they say, put your own oxygen mask on first before trying to help someone put theirs on.

Some of the codependent family behaviors that must be addressed during recovery include keeping secrets, blaming others, ignoring the addiction, normalizing the addiction, and pretending as though nothing has happened.

Codependent Behavior: Keeping Secrets

Keeping secrets is all about dysfunctional ideas of loyalty. My friend Sarah called me one day to tell me that one of her kid's friends drank too much—to the point that the friend had to be carried out of parties and driven home. Sarah's daughter didn't want Sarah to say anything to the friend's mother, so Sarah asked me what I thought she should do. I asked her, "If it was your daughter, would you want to find out that everyone else knew about her drinking and never told you?" Going further, I asked Sarah to envision a scenario in which the friend's daughter ended up in an accident or died. How would she feel facing the girl's parents, knowing she had never said anything to them before?

It's easy to hide behind the thought that it isn't my place to say anything because it doesn't involve my family member. But as we say in the world of recovery: we are only as sick as our secrets. Real friends tell the truth to each other and are not afraid to risk a few hurt feelings. If someone could potentially be hurt or is hurting others, it's wise to speak up.

Another level of secret-keeping is in the family itself. It's not unheard of for a family to have skeletons in the closet that are kept hidden from the younger generations. This is done for a number of reasons and none of them are healthy. More often than not, the family has learned to keep the skeletons hidden due to the shame that the story brings forth. This is the old "What would people say?" syndrome. The rationale is that it is best to keep the skeletons hidden and present the prettiest front. In my business, we call this denial.

The next excuse is, "It is no one else's business," and this is driven by the same shame: "We don't want the neighbors to know because then what will they think of us?"

My favorite excuse is: "Well, that was so long ago, I didn't think it was relevant to today."

This is all about hiding the skeleton way in the back of the closet and acting as if nothing ever happened. And if it did happen, then it is not really relevant to what we are dealing with today. This is just not so! Everything is relevant to the current situation. Addiction and codependency are generational family issues that have ripple effects and create traits that are passed down from generation to generation.

Codependent Behavior: The Blame Game

The blame game can start pretty quickly among individuals who prefer keeping secrets. This often sounds something like, "If you think my family member is bad, you should hear what people say about your family member!"

This is just a defensive comment. A person can always sit down with the friend and explain, "Look, none of our families are perfect, and none of us are perfect, but I am concerned about your kid. (Or sibling, spouse, parent, etc.) If I were you, I would want to know. If you need help, please let me know. We are all in this together."

This is a lot more effective than gossip and brings the focus back to family, friendship, and community. Blaming others is a deflective and defensive act because you then behave as if you are the victim and someone else is at fault. By doing this, you are removing the responsibility of the situation from yourself and placing it on someone else. In this way, you are absolving yourself of taking active steps to prevent or change it. If you are not at fault, it is not your job to do the work to change.

Addressing a family's addiction issues means that all family members understand the individual role they play in it. Not once has someone visited my office and been entirely surprised by their family member's substance use and abuse. In each scenario, the family always knew about it, thought it was no big deal, or believed someone else was addressing the issue. Thus, the blame game begins. The substance abuse becomes society's fault, work's fault, school's fault, the boss's fault, the friend's fault, or the girlfriend's fault. But if your family member is making poor choices in friends, activities, and the people they spend time around, it is your responsibility to set a boundary, not act as though you are helpless to stop it. While you cannot bully your family member into making good decisions, you can counsel and advise them.

As we discussed earlier in the book, use boundaries, accountability and structure on their behavior. If you don't like the people your family member has been hanging out with, set a firm boundary with them. Make it very clear there will be no hanging out with individuals who are using drugs and alcohol. Instruct your family member to account for their time, answer the phone when you text or call, and explain you will be giving random drug tests to ensure your loved one is not using substances. Then, if your family member cannot or will not account for her time, ignores you if you call or text, or does not submit to random drug testing, you will remove privileges (if they are a kid/teen), or remove access to the family (if they are an adult).

View this as an opportunity to talk and listen. Don't lecture; instead, say that you are concerned about your family member's choices and want to know what's going on. Ask about your loved one's life and be available to them on their terms. Talk about what they want to talk about, and listen.

Learning to Listen

One of the biggest mistakes I see repeatedly in my practice is that people won't listen when a family member is telling them about their lives. Instead, they are already forming opinions and judgements of their actions. And most often, that family member will stop sharing information. Consider the Speaker-Listener method (see appendix explaining this method). Overall, the speaker talks and the listener listens, and then repeats what the speaker says back to them. This is not an opportunity to prove that you are right and they are wrong; this is a chance to listen and connect.

Addicts are always telling me that they do talk to their families, but the families just don't listen to them or hear what they are saying. I have watched so many clients interact with their addicted loved ones, and I can see what they're doing. Instead of listening, they're formulating their response or their argument to show how they are right and their addicted family member is wrong. One of the most important things a person can do is listen to their loved one, and acknowledge their feelings and emotions. Listening doesn't mean agreeing or conceding a point. It's just an act of respect.

Codependent Behavior: Normalizing Poor Behavior

Ignoring and normalizing substance abuse another common behavior among families with addiction. I often hear statements such as, "All of the other husbands drink and use drugs; it's no big deal!" or, "You drink and used pot, you told me you did when you were my age, don't be a hypocrite!"

It's okay to be a hypocrite in this situation. Just because you drank or used drugs, it does not make it okay for your family member to do the same thing. If your family member has a substance abuse issue, then you may want to consider your own drinking and drug use, not necessarily because you have a problem, but because it is hard to look at your loved one and tell them to stop when you are not willing to do the same thing.

It is a sign of support to tell your family member who is in treatment that you are willing to support them by looking at your own personal drinking and drug use. This move is all about showing your loved one that they are not in this alone. This is an act of support and love. Creating an atmosphere of honesty and vulnerability in the family is the antidote for all of the negative byproducts of substance abuse.

You do not have to accept that your family member drinks or uses drugs and that these things are necessary for them to fit in or to have a social life.

Working on Codependency

All of the behaviors listed above: keeping secrets, refusing to accept responsibility, and failing to allow your family member to determine their own behavior are all acts of codependency. Other actions can also contribute to this unhealthy dynamic, such as providing addicts with financial assistance to keep them from getting into more trouble, backing down when active substance use is happening, and making excuses for a loved one's behavior are all symptoms of codependency. If you're wondering about being a codependent, ask yourself:

- Do I spend an equal amount of time on each child?

- How's my health?

- How's my mental health?

- How's work?

- How's my marriage?

- Do I eat well?

- Does the addict in my family interfere with any of the above?

I find that getting a codependent family member to address their codependency is literally the same thing as getting the addict to treatment. The key is to get to the point where you can say, *my life isn't working. I need help.* Step back and look at what is going on, because addiction and codependency tend to go together like peanut butter and jelly. Unfortunately, codependent family members are often very resistant to change, because they believe they are the only ones keeping the trains running on time, and are even rewarded for it. When I point out codependent behavior, I often hear defensive statements such as, "Everybody does this!" or, "You're telling me not to be a good mom!" But the addicted loved one is never going to change unless everyone changes—

unless the codependency is broken and there is a willingness to let go. This doesn't mean you cannot provide help and support, when a loved one *asks* for help. But you need to draw a line somewhere.

I have listed books in the last chapter of this book that I encourage all families with addiction to read. More than a few of them center around codependency: what it looks like, how to recognize it in yourself and others, and what to do to break the cycle of codependent behavior so that you and your loved one can move forward together in a healthier, happier and more supportive sober environment. Codependents Anonymous meetings can also be very helpful for the family members of addicts.

Consistency, Transparency, Accountability

As I mentioned in my Author Note at the beginning of the book, I see my work with families as a business consultant would see her work with a company in trouble. It is my job, as your consultant, to do two things: to help each family member understand that they have to change the system because it isn't working, and to empower the individuals in the family to do this themselves. Just as it would be a waste of time to bring in a business consultant to advise your company and then ignore her, it would be a waste of time to bring me in to help your family and discount my message.

As the family member of the addict, it's not your job to change the addict. It's your job to change the system. To do so, we need to see consistency, transparency, and accountability. These three things are like kryptonite to the addict and to the codependent. Let's define what they mean in this context:

- Consistency: Attending regular meetings, regularly.
- Transparency: Everything is on the table. That's a big transition for addicts and codependents. Approach conversations with no agenda.
- Accountability: Alcoholics who show up late and flirt with others in meetings? They will drink again. Accountability means you have a sponsor; you take your recovery seriously. You are that student who sits at the front of the class. It means people notice when you are not at meetings because you are accountable to them.

KEY TAKEAWAYS:

- Codependency is a common concurrent theme in families with addiction, and it easily becomes an issue for all family members.

- Some of the family behaviors that must be addressed during recovery include keeping secrets, blaming others, ignoring the addiction, normalizing the addiction, and pretending as though nothing has happened.

- Just because the addict is in treatment doesn't mean everything is okay. That's just the first step in healing the family.

- You cannot expect your family to succeed after treatment if the family system has not changed.

- Consider attending meetings for Codependents Anonymous, Al-Anon Family Groups or Adult Children of Alcoholics and Dysfunctional Families to change the family system.

WORKSHEET

Symptoms of Codependency Checklist

Please read through this list of codependency symptoms and think about your own life. Put a checkmark next to the ones that apply to you. This material is adapted from psychcentral.com.

- [ ] Low self-esteem: Feeling that you're not good enough or comparing yourself to others are signs of this symptom

- [ ] People-pleasing. Do you go out of your way and sacrifice your own needs to accommodate other people?

- [ ] Poor boundaries. If you have weak boundaries, you feel responsible for other people's feelings and problems. Rigid boundaries mean you are closed off and withdrawn, making it hard for other people to get close.

- [ ] Reactivity. Do you react to everyone's thoughts and feelings, automatically believing them or becoming defensive?

- [ ] Caretaking. If someone else has a problem, you want to help them to the point that you give up yourself.

- [ ] Control. Codependents need to control those close to them, because they need other people to behave in a certain way to feel okay.

- [ ] Dysfunctional communication. You're afraid to be truthful, because you don't want to upset someone else.

- [ ] Obsessions. Codependents have a tendency to spend their time thinking about other people or relationships.

- [ ] Dependency. Do you need other people to like you to feel okay? You may be afraid of being rejected or abandoned,

- [ ] Denial. You don't face your problem or think the problem is someone else or the situation. You may also deny your own feelings and needs.

- [ ] Problems with intimacy. Can you be open and close with someone in an intimate relationship?

- [ ] Painful emotions. Codependency creates stress and leads to painful emotions such as anger and resentment, depression, hopelessness, and despair. This can lead to feeling numb.

Self-Care Checklist

Are you engaging in self-care while your family member is at a treatment center? To hold yourself accountable, consult this checklist on a regular basis:

- [ ] Have I exercised today?

- [ ] Am I eating a nutritious diet?

- [ ] Have I meditated today?

- [ ] Am I attending regular therapy sessions?

chapter seven

HEALING THE
FAMILY SYSTEM

Chapter 7

Healing the Family System

The most important work I do happens in the family system as a whole. We have to break codependency to heal the system. The idea that through my self-sacrifice, I can manipulate you into changing your behavior and your patterns is not healthy or sustainable. It just doesn't work. I see a lot of parents of addicts and spouses of addicts putting themselves out, running interference, solving the problems, taking care of them, bailing them out, getting the lawyers, fighting with the schools…and the object of all that attention is just sitting there, not even caring.

It can be confusing, particularly for the parents of addicted children (of any age). When children are small, of course, it *is* your responsibility to take care of them. But as they get older, your involvement has to decrease. You have to allow them to learn how to solve their own problems, fight their own battles. I always get parents saying things like, "I don't understand, when I was 30 years old, I paid my own bills! Why can't my son?" I say, "Well, why should he? You keep doing it!"

The essence of this whole discussion is the members of the family learning to let go. And allowing the addict to actually get into trouble. Kick them out of the nest and see if they fly. I understand that you may feel that if you don't keep caretaking the addict in your family, they will die, and that's why you keep perpetuating the system, thinking, "At least my struggling loved one is still alive." But this way of operating is simply not sustainable long-term. Sometimes they're going to hit a few branches on the way down, but that's how they learn. Unfortunately, one of the reasons that codependent family members focus on the addict is they don't want to look at themselves. They don't want to address their own stuff. They don't want to take a look at their part of the situation. It's easier to blame others for not following through than it is to change yourself.

It becomes necessary to go back to what we talked about and the first part of the book: are you really ready to change? Have you really tried everything else? And has it worked? No? Okay, then it is time to do things differently. Because going back to that old place where you start meddling, you start trying to fix everything, manage everything? That's not going to work. But change is hard. The codependent role has been passed down generationally. This is not new. Once people start to see this, and they start to address their issue and their compulsive desire to constantly fix and take care of and solve, they often say things like, "Oh, crap, this is what my mom was like." When we see the pattern, we can change the pattern—the people-pleasing, the defensiveness, the denial.

When the family stops trying to solve and fix and take care of things, that's when the addict realizes they're going to have to get help. But that's the hard part for the family. It scares them. They say, "I'd rather have this wounded animal living in my basement then go out in the wild and not come back." But you're not alone. Treatment is the bridge to a better way of life for your family. And when your addicted family member is in treatment, the whole system has the chance to evolve.

In the beginning, every time we have a family session or an individual session with the family members, we spend half the time talking about the addict. And I'll go along with that for a couple of sessions. But then, I'll point out to the person I'm working with, "Do you realize we're spending all of our time talking about him?" I know we've finally made some progress in the family when we stop talking about the addict.

Questions Families Ask Me

Q: How can I best support my family member's recovery?

A: Get into your own recovery. Nothing will change the relationship more than your own recovery. Also consider 12 step recovery, CODA, ALANON or NARANON. Try them out and see which one fits you. Read books on codependency and family systems and ultimately, educate yourself on addiction and codependency. Some resources that can help:

- Codependent No More by Melody Beattie
- Chronic Hope: Parenting the Addicted Child by Kevin Petersen
- Daring Greatly by Brené Brown (also watch her TED Talks from 2010 (Vulnerability) and 2012 (Shame) on vulnerability and shame. These will help you understand what your family member is experiencing.

- Parenting Teens with Love and Logic by Cline and Fay – It doesn't matter if your family member in treatment is 16, 26, 36 or 46 this book will help you with setting boundaries and preparing for when they leave treatment.

- "Pleasure Unwoven" by Kevin McCauley – This documentary is a great resource for families to understand the medical science of addiction as well as the psychological.

Also feel free to attend the treatment center's family weekend and weekly family meetings and share your experiences with the other families or ask questions if you need help or support.

Q: What do I say when our family member is in treatment?

A: It's normal to wonder, 'What do we tell our friends and family?' You don't have to keep secrets anymore and you're not obligated to share anything with anyone that you don't want to. If someone is asking about your family member, tell them to ask them directly, not ask you about them. It's not your story to tell.

Q: How involved should we be in their treatment?

A: It is totally reasonable to receive updates from the therapist and the case manager and to participate in family therapy. The Sponsor is for the person in recovery and that is not for the family to be involved with, however you may end up meeting them if your family member chooses to introduce you to them.

Q: Should we allow the addict to make mistakes and not solve their problem?

A: Yes, that's how they learn. Every time you rescue him, you are robbing him of a chance to learn from his mistakes. "No" is a complete sentence. The hardest part for the family is standing back and watching and not rescuing.

Q: What do we do if they relapse? Do we have to take them back?

A: Hold the same boundaries you did when they entered treatment. Tell them, "We love you and if you want to get sober, we will help you. If you don't want to get sober then we still love you but we are going to choose to have boundaries." Only keep paying for treatment if you can afford it and want to. You can be okay whether they are sober or not.

Q: What do we do when they call with problems and issues with the treatment center?

A: That sounds like something you should talk to your therapist/case manager or sponsor about and determine how you're going to deal with that. Remember: we have to heal the family system just like we have to heal the addict. You are not responsible for your family member's addiction, but you are responsible for how you respond to it. Addiction has a ripple effect in the family and creates trauma for everyone involved.

Q: Does addiction ever go away or does the addict get healed?

A: The reality is that if you are an addict, you are always an addict and will always need to treat your addiction. The good news is that being sober and in recovery is awesome and fun! Recovery is not a chore or a sentence to being miserable for the rest of your life.

Q: Where do you draw the line between helping someone and being codependent?

A: Ask yourself, "Is this something my family member is capable of solving themselves?" If the answer is yes, you need to let them take care of it. Even if they do poorly. That is how they learn. Help is the sunny side of control, so you have to be careful.

Q: Do we have to keep supporting them financially while they are in treatment?

A: Part of the process of recovery is learning how to solve your own problems and take responsibility for yourself financially, which can be a gradual process. It's reasonable to expect to get paid back. Part of the process of making amends (9th step) is to ask what they can do to set things right and it's okay to ask for a monthly payment plan. It's about the process of taking responsibility and gaining some self- esteem. The payments can be small and nominal, it's the action that matters.

Q: What do we do if they cause problems with the treatment center?

A: Say, "That sounds like something you should talk to your therapist/case manager or sponsor about and determine how you're going to deal with that." Remember, "No" is a complete sentence. The hardest part for the family is standing back and watching and not rescuing. Remember: we have to heal the family system just like we have to heal the addict. You are not responsible for your family member's addiction, but you are responsible for how you respond to it. Addiction has a ripple effect in the family and creates trauma for everyone involved.

Q: How should we behave when we visit or when they come home?

A: Consult your family therapist before they come home. You don't have to stop drinking because they do: Part of recovery is reintegrating into the real world. If they become uncomfortable, they can speak up or they can always leave.

Q: Why do we have to attend meetings or therapy?

A: Addiction has a ripple effect in the family and creates trauma for everyone involved. We have to heal the family system just like we have to heal the addict. This creates the best chance for long term recovery. You are not responsible for your family member's addiction, but you are responsible for how you respond to it.

Unwinding Family Trauma Responses

To give you more insight into the work the entire family can engage in while their loved one is in treatment, I consulted my friend Michael F. Barnes, PhD., MAC, LPC. Mike is the Chief Clinical Officer at Foundry Treatment Center in Steamboat Springs, Colorado. To learn more about the work they do, visit ForgingNewLives.com. He is also an expert in the area of family traumatology and does a lot of work with families who experience secondary trauma as the result of addiction.

"The family gets their loved one in treatment, and they have a moment of respite," Mike said. "They're catching their breath, and they often think, 'He's the one that has the problem. I just wish my loved one would get sober so that we can go back to normal.' And what they miss is [addiction] is not an acute illness where someone gets sick in a week. They're getting sick over the course of months to years. This loved one was a member of your family, and they developed a chronic, progressive, and potentially fatal illness. And it didn't just happen out of the blue."

Mike explains that there are familial factors that play into this chronic disease progression. As a person slowly gets more and more advanced in their illness, the family system shifts to accommodate them. So, by the time that individual gets into treatment, the family is usually in as much denial as the addicted person. Family members don't want to deal with the pain of having to look at their own father and his alcoholism, or their own mother, for example, as someone with chronic depression, suicidality, or severe trauma.

But family history and family systems are crucial to acknowledge and examine.

"My research has been on the secondary trauma of parents of children who require an intensive care treatment—hospitalization," Mike explained. "For example, I have a son who was hit by a car when he was five. He just turned 34. Our entire family got traumatized by that event and the term that we use is 'organized around,' which means his well-being became the focus of our lives. And there are then all these other things that don't get done."

The family organization is the set of unspoken rules or daily routines informed by the parents' experience of the world. Mike's clients are very concerned about going home after their time in a treatment center for addiction, because they believe it's going to be a really difficult transition. They fear that they'll never live up to their family's expectations.

"I use the example of a mobile over a baby's crib." Mike explained. "As each piece is moving, it dissipates the energy so it can flow back into a state of homeostasis. The weights that balance it out are what allows it to be able to tolerate being disturbed. Each piece responds to the motion of the other parts. So, as the addiction disease is getting worse, the mobile configuration is shifting to be able to still be balanced with this member who's really struggling. Everyone's reacting to everyone else. If the family doesn't shift to accommodate the person who goes to treatment, there's a problem when they return home. Suddenly, they have opinions about things. Suddenly, they are setting boundaries on what they need to do to stay sober. And a lot of times families struggle with that, particularly after everything they've done for their loved one. They think, 'Now *you're* going to start telling *us* what we need to do?'"

Mike says there are three potential outcomes when a family faces addiction:

- *The addicted person changes and the family changes.* That person's likelihood of getting and staying sober is significantly higher in this scenario because there's lots of support. The family is more resilient, they're really seeing it as "our problem that we all have." This is the best-case scenario,

- *The addict changes but the family doesn't.* When the addict returns home from treatment, and everyone else is still treating them the same way they treated them before, then that person is either going to relapse or leave and get their social support somewhere else, often from AA and the 12-Step community.

- *The family does make changes yet the client becomes chronic in their illness and the family moves on.* When you think of chronic disease management, Mike explained, there are three phases. The first is the crisis phase and that's generally as the illness is progressing. There's been no treatment yet; there's never been a diagnosis. Then, there's the chronic phase, which is living with the chronic illness, and then unfortunately there's the termination phase. And that's when the person becomes incredibly ill. Addiction is a potentially fatal illness. 128 people die from opioid overdose every day in the United States; 240 die from alcohol abuse.

Building a More Resilient Family Unit

Family healing comes from the willingness to engage in difficult conversations. A family who has committed to this process of change will be able to have truly honest communication. And that's the key to the whole thing: becoming a little more fearless and breaking the rules of *don't talk about it. Don't allow yourself to experience your feelings. Don't trust them.*

"From my research, family members are actually more traumatized than their addicted loved one because they're the ones who are trying to keep the lid on everything," Mike said. "And so, they have intrusive thoughts, they have nightmares, they don't sleep. They avoid and ruminate: 'Is my loved one okay? Did they get to a doctor's appointment?' All this hyper-vigilance and the need to control everything is a trauma response. What they will find, as the family healing occurs, is that their nervous system can relax. They can begin to live their own lives."

If family members—if you—can begin this process that allows you to have different relationships, not only with the addict but with all of your family members, the overall health of the family improves.

"The family has to take the client out of the middle," Mike concludes. "If they can do that then the relationships between all of those family members gets better. Their autonomic nervous system will begin to relax. They won't be in fight or flight mode. They'll be able to joke and laugh and have meaningful conversations. They'll be able to get their own needs met, rather than worrying about 'What's going to happen if I die, and he doesn't get sober?' What we're trying to get our families to do is, again, accept responsibility for dealing with the situation as a family, rather than, 'it's just his problem.'"

Another marker of progress? Increased tolerance and patience for each other. This person is still going to have moments where he drives everybody crazy, but can you increase patience? Finally, decreased hyper-vigilance is a great goal to set. How long does it take, when your loved one returns to the house, for you to think, "I need to look to make sure he is okay?" The answer with hundreds and hundreds of families, Mike noted, is: about two seconds. Hyper-vigilance is a trauma response; the families of addicted loved ones experience a shift in the nervous system. And it can take a long time to decrease that hot set-point. But it must be done. Otherwise, your loved one will return home and think, "People are still treating me like I'm using. I'm still not really a member of the family."

More on the Role of Trauma in Codependency and Addiction

As Mike Barnes helped us understand earlier in this chapter, it is very common for trauma to play a role in family codependency and addiction recovery. We only have space in this book for a somewhat brief additional discussion of this complex issue, so I encourage you to seek out additional resources regarding trauma treatment. To offer the best possible overview, I consulted with a therapist in Bend, Oregon who is a leader in working with families on addiction and trauma issues. Brennon Patrick Moore, MS, CTT, CADC-II, LPC is the co-founder of SkylineRecoveryBend.com.

"One of the biggest things families struggle to appreciate is transgenerational trauma, the patterns that get passed down from family to family," Brennon said. For example, he was recently working with a young man with a mental health diagnosis and addiction, and could not effectively treat this individual without treating his mother, who struggled with the same mental health issue most of her life as well. She had a lot of fear that she would project onto him stemming from abuse she had experienced. They had to take a look at how long abuse like that had been happening in this family; the mother suspected it went all the way back several generations.

The point of the work Brennon does, and the work that I do, is to help a whole family understand that the problem isn't just the loved one who happens to be in an addiction treatment facility right now. That's the common misconception. The person who struggles with addiction becomes the "identified patient," and the rest of the family, if it is not careful, can tell a story that this person is the only issue. This is such a common fallacy, which is why I keep bringing it up.

The family piece is crucial to healing addiction, codependency, and trauma, so the task is to create time and space in which each member can zoom out and look at the whole picture, and the whole history. Sometimes, a family is not willing to do this, and it makes it incredibly difficult for the addicted person to then stay sober—because nothing has changed when they return home from treatment. Thirty-day treatment is only the beginning—the real work happens from day 31 through day 365 and beyond.

Shame is a big barrier for addicts and for their families. Sometimes families don't want to look at what's going on because it can be pretty difficult to reckon with—abuse, abandonment, other instances of addiction or historical trauma. When families don't want to dig in and make changes, the therapist's job is to work with addicted individuals to create boundaries when they emerge from treatment and keep the family at a distance. Trauma treatment requires a person feeling safe and willing to explore.

"Trauma lives in the body. It's a visceral experience," Brennon said. "And so, if we're not able to help our clients who have pre-existing

PTSD or pre-existing trauma, we put a Band-Aid on the symptoms but the real root cause underneath is never going to be resolved. The research shows abuse ages a child's DNA. One of the things that you'll often hear about trauma survivors is they're 'old before their time.' Maybe they were taking care of mom and their siblings when they were still children themselves. Or maybe they're only 19, yet they're already jaded and hopeless about the fate of the world or their potential for the future.

"This is why trauma work is so important. You can send somebody to treatment, and when there's yoga classes and food being made for them and a labyrinth that they can walk on and beautiful views and all this kind of stuff, they're going to do great. They're going to feel good because they are in an artificial environment. That environment is important for healing, but when they go out into the real world, where parents are still sick and not willing to do their own work, or where there's COVID-19 and crazy political stuff and protests on the street...all this stuff is incredibly triggering. Their body is going to get activated and they're not going to know what to do with it."

Trauma changes a person's perception of the world in ways that cannot and should not be ignored. Brennon explained that the psychiatrist Bessel van der Kolk did a piece of research with kids at the University of

Boston that's relevant to the discussion here. Dr. van der Kolk had a control group and experimental group of children. One group consisted of traumatized children and one group of non-traumatized children. He showed pictures out of magazines to the two groups. One picture was this brother and sister working on a car with their dad, and the brother is passing a hammer to a sister. The dad's underneath smiling. The doctor would ask the two groups, "What do you think happens in a scene like this? What do you think happens next?"

The non-traumatized kids said wonderful things like, "They will go to McDonald's and get Happy Meals for lunch." The traumatized kids said things like, "I bet you that jack falls out from underneath the car and crushes the dad." Or, "That little girl is about to smash her brother's head with the hammer." We know that trauma changes not only a person's DNA, but re-wires their central nervous system as well. It changes their perception of what they think is going to happen next in the world. For somebody who struggles with addiction, this is important to understand, because the whole point of addiction recovery is trying to convince people that they can make amends for past wrongs, heal their past hurts, and rebuild their lives. But if they have significant trauma, there's this wounded voice in their minds, typically a younger part of them, that is in the background saying "No, you're going to suffer forever. This is the way it is."

Trauma survivors who are also addicts, Brennon noted, almost all say the same thing: "I did well for a few months, then the negative self-talk started to leak in." Then, they relapse. Thus, we cannot ignore things like the ACE study, the adverse childhood experience study conducted in the 1990s at Kaiser Permanente of thousands of people. It showed approximately 85% of all individuals who struggle with addiction had significant trauma histories. Young men, for example, with a score of six or higher (meaning they had six or more adverse childhood experiences) had a 4,600% increase in their probability of IV drug use. The correlation between trauma and substance use is clear.

For families who are committed to healing codependency and trauma, the first step is simply for everybody to commit to doing their own work, to agree that this isn't just going to be something that's dumped on the person in addiction treatment, or passed off to be done later.

"The family needs to go to a retreat or an intensive," Brennon advised. "Everybody needs to be on the same page, because one of the key things about trauma is that *you don't feel safe in your world*. And one of the things that helps that client feel safe is when they see the entire family system making an effort to get better. The other thing that I recommend is that everybody do work focused on something deeper than just talk therapy. I'm not anti-cognitive behavioral therapy, but the research on its effectiveness for trauma is really not there.

"What is shown to be effective is body-based modalities like Somatic Experience, yoga, art therapy. People make a mistake regarding a trauma when they think they can just talk about it and it'll get better. It's the old idea of catharsis, that the therapist is going to have some sort of insight, as in, 'You date these kinds of men because it's your father,' and then you're like, 'Oh my God, I get it!' But it just doesn't work that way. The way trauma works is when we experience something that tells our brain and body, 'I could die!' it causes a cortisol spike in our brain that leaves a permanent change in our neuro-synaptic connectivity. It changes the way our brain is wired."

It's like if you had a house with smoke alarms that went off when you open the doors. You would have to go in and rewire the system. You can't just go in there and walk around and talk about it. So, the commitment to doing some stuff that is going to make you uncomfortable is the key. Brennon explained that while we love to talk, as a culture, to actually go into deeper level work is really important.

None of this is easy. "Whenever clients come and say, 'I don't know if I can do this,' I always just let them know *this is hard*," Brennon said. "It takes such courage to even just be sitting in my office. As therapists, I think it's critical we disclose a little bit about ourselves. So, I often share part of my own story and some of my own work I've done. I think it's important that our clients know our human-ness.

"I also let them know that they're in complete control regarding the speed we go. I don't think a trauma survivor should ever be forced in anything. Trauma work should be aggressive and sensitive all at the same time. I think you should be focused and you should be moving forward, doing assignments, doing active work like EMDR or brain-spotting or art therapy. But if a client can't tolerate it. It doesn't matter what your agenda is. Go slow. EMDR, for example, can be very intense. I think that's important is to pace it in a way that makes the client feel safe."

KEY TAKEAWAYS:

- For an addict to change, the entire family has to change. We call this "healing the family system."

- Inter-generational trauma often plays a role in codependency and addiction and should be treated by a therapist with expertise in this area.

- Hyper-vigilance on the part of a family member is a trauma response.

- As the family member of an addict, you can and should also do the work of the 12 steps. For extra help with this, please see Appendix 7 at the end of this book.

My Self-Care Plan

☐ Therapy:

_____

_____

_____

☐ Exercise:

_____

_____

_____

☐ Nutrition:

_____

_____

_____

☐ Meditation:

_____

_____

_____

☐ Community:

_____

_____

_____

☐ 12-Step Meetings:

_____

_____

_____

Part Three

After Treatment

1. Discuss reintegration plan for all family members.

2. Outline family member expectations.

3. Seek a family therapist who specializes in codependency and addiction therapy.

chapter eight

REINTRODUCTION

Chapter 8

Reintegration

Your loved one comes home from treatment, whether it's 30, 60, 90 days, or a year. They're on track, but the family starts to drop the ball or act like, "It's not that big of a deal. We don't have to go to therapy." Now we're in the homestretch. This is where Dr. McCauley's 10-step plan (found in the appendix), becomes so important. The initial thing we like to see is at least 30 days of residential treatment then a seamless transition into a sober living environment. From there, we go to frequent non-random drug testing and an outpatient treatment program and the relapse prevention program. Now, we're bringing the person home. So, we have gotten through the first stage of, "oh my god there's an addict in the house. What do we do!" We've tried plan A, it failed, we went to plan B, an intervention and treatment. They went to treatment for X amount of time, and now it's time for them to come home.

Remember, there are two tracks here. There's the addict, and there is the family. Generally, what the family will devolve back to is, "What are we going to do to make the addict okay?" My response to that question is, "No. Just as the addict needs to go to treatment, so does the family." While the addict is in treatment, it's critical that the family has gone to therapy, read all the books about codependency, started 12 step meetings, and started their own recovery. Repeat after me: *the best way for me to support my family member in recovery is get into my own recovery.*

The reason why becomes apparent, because now we're bringing everybody back together. We have got to make sure that the system has changed. Not that the addict has changed. Instead, it's making sure the system has changed. And the system entails the addict and all the family members.

What that looks like is having a plan. What's the recovery plan for the addict? What's the recovery plan for the family members? Here is what I suggest:

1. Attending regular meetings, regularly

2. Individual therapy for each family member

3. Couples or family therapy

4. Consistently good nutrition as well as regular exercise and meditation, or some sort of relaxation or spirituality practice

5. Have fun as a family

Finally, have some sort of incentive as well. One of the things Dr. McCauley talks about is you got to schedule in fun. So, let's make that number five. You've got to have fun as a family. Some good examples are a family movie night, it can be a date night, doing something silly with the kids, going to the park, let the kid run the show. Let them pick the movie, let them pick the food. Go out an hour-long walk, but not a not a power walk, but just a relaxed walk. You have to plan for some sort of engaged fun, so that everybody's not standing around waiting for the addict to screw up again. What I hear all the time is, "I'm just waiting for the other shoe to drop. I'm waiting for the phone call."

When I hear family members say that, what they're telling me is, "I'm not taking care of my own recovery." They're not doing their own work. One of the one of the things I always say is, "You could be okay, whether they're sober or not." If you're working on your own recovery, you can get to a place where you're neutral.

Neutral is a critical term and it looks like this: "I'm going to go to my Al-Anon meeting. I'm going to go to my therapy. I'm going to go to the gym. I'm going to eat well; I'm not going to smoke cigarettes. I'm not going to get high, I'm not going to get drunk. I'm going to take care of myself. If you choose not to, that's cool. That's your choice but then my choice is to go back to Plan A."

This means, for example, that Dad comes home from treatment and everybody is taking care of their own business. Mom's going to Al-Anon. She's got a sponsor, she's working the steps, she's going to therapy. She's going to the gym; she's taking care of herself. Dad comes home doing all the same stuff, and we all live happily ever after. And it happens. It happens because happy families come from happy individuals, and happy individuals work on their stuff.

Here's the deal: stuff is going to happen. Regular, everyday stuff is going to occur. Things are going to get tough at work, things are going to get tough at school, things are going to get tough in the family. So, you have to have that muscle prepared. Just as you've got to go to the gym to get healthy, you've got to flex the mental health muscle as well, so that when crisis hits, you're not already at a 12. You're down at a four or five, thinking, "We can handle this. We have the resources. I have a sponsor, I have a therapist; we have a couple's therapist, and we have a plan. And we're going to address the issue within the structure of the plan."

Whether you have followed Plan A and your family member has found success, or you have gone through the struggle of Plan B and your loved one is now out of rehab, what can you do to help them stay focused on their sobriety? What resources might be out there that can help both you and your family member along this new path?

One of the most important lessons to take away from this book and your recent experience is that you should never expect your loved one to do something you would be unwilling to do. Provide your family member with an example of the type of behavior you would like to see from him. For example, if you would like your family member to attend regular therapy sessions, you should also make an appointment with a therapist. If your goal is to have your loved one attend 12 Step meetings in your area, make sure you are attending meetings meant for the families and addressing their issues.

Aside from setting an example, additional follow-up methods can also assist you in learning what the next span of time might look like for you and for your loved one. Being clean and staying sober are new experiences for an addict. Often, the addiction has kept them from facing reality and their issues, and now there is no buffer between them and their problems. In some cases, this shock to the system can lead to relapse for an addict and a fallback into old, familiar patterns for their families.

Avoid Old Patterns and Behaviors

How do you avoid these? It starts with seeking both individual and family therapy. Include everyone who lives in your household in these family sessions, as they have experienced living with and loving an addict and they will likely need some guidance about what to do next.

Just because the addict is now clean and sober does not mean that the problem has been solved and everything will now be "normal." All "being clean" means is that the crisis you all faced together is now over. Now, it is time for you all to address the family patterns that you have become comfortable with and learn how to change them, in order to move forward. Old patterns will no longer apply, so learning new ways to deal with stress, difficulty, static amongst family members and any other problems that may arise will be keys to success.

Make sure that whatever therapy model and therapist you choose fully addresses both the addiction your loved one went through and the codependency you, as their family member, experienced. Spend some time getting to know your provider to determine whether they are the one for you. Make sure they are knowledgeable on both addiction and codependency. Ask them about the method of recovery you and your family member have chosen, and ensure that they are well-versed in it.

The worst thing families can do when they are dealing with a newly clean addict is to bring them back into a family dynamic that has not changed. Your loved one's reasons for using drugs or alcohol may stem from the home. And in many instances, this is true. If the home does not change, then nor will the urge to use. If the family system does not go through an overhaul after the upheaval of implementing Plan A or Plan B, you will more than likely find yourself back in the same crisis you were in when you picked up this book. Avoid this recipe for disaster by doing the legwork and getting yourself, your loved one, and your entire family familiar with the difficult work that lies ahead.

Most of the families who find success when they work with me are the ones who are willing to do the hard work of continuing to grow, evolve, and change their behaviors and patterns after their loved one leaves the rehabilitation center or halfway house. They are willing to read all of the books I suggest to them when we are working together. The books I recommend deal with both of the problems: addiction and codependency.

These successful families are also willing to continue working in a therapeutic environment, both on their own, with their family member who is now in recovery, and with the other members of their family who have also been affected by the addiction. The addicts, themselves, make the decision and commitment to attend AA, NA, or CA or another support group meeting, while their families find their own support meetings, such as ACA, Al-Anon, Codependency Anonymous, and attend with as much regularity as the addict.

Each individual involved is willing to work the steps or engage in a spiritual practice that helps them to change their behaviors. These spiritual practices change from person to person, depending on their faith and what they feel the most comfortable with, and can range from taking yoga classes and learning to meditate to finding a spiritually-based group and connecting with the message and people in it.

Stick with It

For both the addict and the codependent, I have two conditions they need to meet before they move forward with other forms of therapy and addiction management (such as therapy or AA). The first is that the addiction and the family disease must be under control. Neither behavior can change if it has not reached a full stop first. When someone stops drinking, for example, they do not do so by slowly pouring half an ounce less into their glass over time. To quit a behavior as ingrained as addiction or codependency, it must first stop being the only behavior that either party knows.

Secondly, behavior must change. As it turns out, this is usually the hardest part, which can come as a surprise to some people who have gone through the difficult, sometimes agonizing process of implementing all of Plan B. However, it can be easier to change certain things about ourselves when we are in an environment designed to help us stick to the commitment made to change it, such as a treatment center. Designed to turn people away from using, there is 24-hour around the clock support with days and nights highly structured, leaving little room for downtime, boredom, or dwelling on negative or traumatic experiences.

When these environments no longer surround an addict, the urge to use can potentially become overwhelming. For this reason, no one is kidding when they say the road to recovery is a long one. It requires regular work and effort on the part of everyone involved, and that work only occasionally becomes easier with time. When you become involved in the next steps of recovery, it is imperative that you and your loved one commit yourselves fully to the process and stick with it, even when it seems like everything is going swimmingly.

Here is an attitude that *won't* work: "Well, he came home from treatment. He went to an AA meeting and we went to therapy once. We're really busy people, Kevin."

I hear that all the time. Then, somebody starts behaving like they did before. It doesn't even have to be the addict. Sometimes, the addict is the one that digs in and gets his act together, and the family is like, "Whoa! You're behaving differently; we don't like this. You're going to meetings and you're not hanging out with us. You're praying and meditating, we don't like that. And why do *we* have to quit drinking?"

To this, I ask the family, if somebody came home from living in the hospital for 30 days because they were diabetic and almost died, would you then immediately have a big party with cakes and cookies and cupcakes for them? Or would you say, "We're just not going to have sugar in the house because that's life threatening to you." Does that mean you can't eat sugar ever? No. Knock yourself out. But be thoughtful about it.

For an addict, it's not enough to just quit drinking and quit doing drugs. And for their family members, it's not enough to quit being controlling manipulative and codependent. You have to attend to those things and have a plan to stay in recovery. You've got to go to the mental gym: therapy, AA, Al-Anon. You've got to attend to it, and surround yourself with the people that are doing the same thing, fighting the same battle.

The Money Question

The financial piece of the puzzle is a big deal for families. Fortunately, 12 step meetings are free. And if you have insurance, you can find therapists who take your insurance. You can make it work. Almost all treatment programs have an alumni group and alumni meetings that you can engage with.

The resources are all there. It's really about staying engaged. You have to change the way you live in order to accommodate change, to make that happen. You can do it affordably. There are low cost therapy alternatives, but you may have to do a little legwork to find them. You can't sit there and say things like, "Oh, my God. You don't understand!"

When people say that to me, I reply, "So, in other words, you don't want to make an effort."

There is a place in Denver, for example, that has now expanded all over the country. It's called The Phoenix and it is a gym that a buddy of mine, Scott Strode, put together about 10 or 15 years ago. The Phoenix is a nonprofit he created to teach kids coming out of treatment how to mountain bike, how to road bike, how to run, how to swim, how to mountain climb, how to rock climb, how to indoor rock climb, how to ice climb, how to camp. It's free; all you have to do is be sober.

There are these resources available all over the country. But the key is, you have to avail yourself of them; you have to do a little legwork.

System Maintenance

In the perfect world, everybody's doing their own stuff right and taking care of themselves, so that when we bring everybody back together, we've changed the family system. Start with weekly check-ins with a family therapist for maybe the first month or two, and then bi weekly, and then every three weeks and then maybe once a month. During this time, everyone is going to individual therapy and 12 step meetings. It's accessing those resources to continue to make the internal family system change.

Because if nothing changes, nothing changes.

Every time somebody relapses it's for one of two reasons. One, the individual was just like, "I ain't doing it."

If you're going to therapy and a 12-step meeting consistently, and you have a sponsor, and your life doesn't change, then you need to find a new meeting and a new sponsor and a new therapist. If your life isn't changing that's on you, that's not on them. Right. We're in a new era of personal responsibility.

A family no longer gets to point to the addict and say, "It's all his fault." That's over with. We're taking away that excuse and the addict no longer gets to look at the family and say, "See? It's all their fault."

Failing to plan is planning to fail.

When to Return to Work

I understand that the family is like, "Hey, we need you to come back and go to work." But every time that's been the priority, sobriety has always failed.

When I hear, "You don't understand. He has to go back to work. He has to get a job; he has to provide for his family." But in one case in Chicago that I'm remembering, I said, "That's great. Here's what's going to happen. He's going to start using again immediately." And that's what happened. Whatever you put in front of your sobriety, you better be prepared to lose, including your family, your children, your job, your wealth.

If you maintain your sobriety first—and when I say sobriety, I'm talking about the codependency issue also—everything flows. I have 29 years of doing this yet people want to argue with me. I always say, "Knock yourself out. But I'm going to continue to go to my meetings, I'm going to continue to go to therapy; I'm going to continue to take care of myself, because that's what makes me available to be a member of the family, to be married, to be part of the package. Taking care of me."

I know that when I stopped taking care of me, I stopped being part of the family and I stopped being a good husband. I stopped being a good employer.

When the Family System Doesn't Change

The other scenario is the addict will come back from treatment and dig into his sobriety. But he's the only one and he feels like he's on an island, you know, because what happens right is all of a sudden, he starts to get clarity. He starts to see his way of life and he starts to get sane, and he starts looking at his family. He's like, Oh, God, because he sees all of the anxiety, the manipulation, the control, the passive aggressive behavior, the low self-esteem, the people pleasing, the poor boundaries. They're like, "Oh, this is all the stuff they told me to watch out for."

And they're frustrated because they come home and the family system hasn't changed. And it doesn't matter if they're 16, and a kid, or 22, and in college, or 40, and married with kids. It's all the same when the family system hasn't changed. Because the attitude is, "We don't have a problem, you have a problem." And so what I end up recommending to those people is you've got to start setting boundaries. It is not uncommon for people to come back from treatment and get divorced within the first year or two. Because the family system doesn't want to change and the addict and the alcoholic is like, "I've got to change or am I going to go right back to where I was. I can't be part of the system anymore." So, they get divorced or they cheat. Codependents cheat, too.

Relapse

If there is a relapse, you'll have to go back to plan A. Lay it down and say, "Here's the deal: no drugs, no alcohol, you've got to go back to work and you've got to be responsible. We've got to talk about the family behavior at home." Plan A and Plan B come right back into play. "And if you can't, that's cool. But then you got to move out. We can't continue to participate with this." It has to be that black and white.

COVID-19 is making everything harder for families because everyone's contained. We're all under the roof together; we're all on top of each other. It's more difficult to hide problems, everything gets washed out, especially with the kids and the teens, because they can't hide. Mom and Dad aren't even leaving the house to go to work.

Some Books and Videos I Recommend

When families are looking for more information outside of our sessions that may help them move forward with and understand their kid better, I often recommend specific books to them that may help them work through their situation and gain greater insight and understanding into what has been going on in the home.

I am personally a huge advocate of the work of Brené Brown, and I recommend her to all of my clients. She is a research professor at the University of Houston and specializes in studying empathy, courage, shame, and vulnerability. Her stance is that we all must "walk through vulnerability to get to courage," and her viewpoint on vulnerability is refreshing and honest.

I highly suggest at least one viewing of her TED Talk on vulnerability (2010) and shame (2012). Both of these can be found online through her website, as well as on Amazon. I also recommend all of her books, beginning with *Daring Greatly*. Additionally, you can visit her website and find a therapist who utilizes her work, if you find that what she has to say resonates with you and your family member while you are travelling along the road to recovery.

I always believe that every family and addict can benefit from watching *Pleasure Unwoven*, an amazing documentary by Dr. Kevin McCauley. Dr. McCauley explains the biological side of addiction and implements a 10-point plan for recovery that is fundamental for both the addict and the family and he shares his own experiences with his addiction. His second documentary, *Memo to Self*, is as good as the *Pleasure Unwoven* and I think that both should be mandatory.

If the addict in your family is a teen, a book I cannot recommend often enough is *Parenting Teens with Love and Logic*, by Foster Kline, M.D., and Jim Fay. This book was written to help parents prepare their teenagers for what responsible adulthood will be like, and can often be a boon for those parents who feel as though they are underwater when it comes to giving their teen the guidance that they know they need. The goal of the book is to give parents the empowerment they need to set boundaries, impart necessary skills, and encourage positive decision-making skills in their teenager. Topics the authors cover include: ADD, divorce, and addiction, making it a great addition to the family library.

Codependent No More, written by Melanie Beattie, is a gold-standard in self-help and recovery circles. Because so many clients of mine face the issue of codependency alongside their teen's addiction, I generally steer them towards this book, so they can understand why and how this codependency happened and what they can do about it from here on out. Beattie gives readers self-assessment tests and exercises, so they can apply the things they are learning to their own situations. The guidance this book provides is laid out well and is easy to follow, making it a great tool for parents to utilize as they try to fix the codependency that they have developed. She has an updated version, *The New Codependency*, which helps people understand that they don't have to have an active addict in their lives to be suffering from codependency, sometimes dealing with mental health issues or generational trauma can create dysfunctional family patterns as well.

Along the lines of codependency in parents, *Facing Codependence: What It Is, Where It Comes from, How It Sabotages Our Lives* is another great read that can really open the eyes of parents who need a gentle push into understanding how things in their family have unraveled because of codependency. The author, Pia Mellody, gives parents a solid framework for identifying and understanding codependent thinking, behavior, and feelings, as well as a clear list of what codependency looks like. It also gives a lot of insight into what might have started the codependency that a parent can experience, which can go a long way towards breaking the pattern of it.

Alcoholics Anonymous and *Paths to Recovery* are both incredibly useful resources for both parents and addicts. Both address the AA and Al-Anon steps, concepts, and traditions, which can be a great way for parents and teens to both find some help of their own and also read something that gives them insight into what the other is doing and working on. These books are ones I almost always recommend as companion reads for families who are committed to attending meetings.

In the Realm of Hungry Ghosts, by Dr. Gabor Mate, is a great choice of book for anyone who is dealing with addiction, either their own or their child's. The true stories of the things other people have experienced give a good representation of the people who can be affected by addiction. Spoiler alert: it's everyone. It's a useful book to help people understand that addiction is something that can happen to anyone, at any time.

Lastly, I always recommend that clients take a look at a particular landmark study: cdc.gov/violenceprevention/acestudy/ about adverse childhood experiences. The website belongs to the CDC, and there are links to click through explaining the study itself, resources to use to understand the study and the results, and articles that cover a broad range of topics about adverse childhood experiences. This study gives a lot of insight into how things that happen to individuals as children can affect their behavior later in life. It's an incredibly useful study, and I strongly encourage clients to read it to gain more insight into how these types of experiences end up shaping us as teenagers and adults.

KEY TAKEAWAYS:

- The worst thing a family can do when they are dealing with a newly clean addict is to bring them back into a family dynamic that has not changed.

- Happy families come from happy individuals; everyone should be addressing their issues in therapy and 12 step support groups.

- There are lots of great books about families and addiction available. Don't fall into the trap that once the addict is sober everything is all better.

- Consistency, Accountability and Transparency are critical in the sober person's and the family's success.

- Make a plan for when your loved one comes home that includes family therapy, individual therapy, and support groups for everyone, and having fun together as a family.

WORKSHEET

For the Addict.

☐ Regular attendance at AA meetings

☐ Regular individual therapy for each family member

☐ Regular couples or family therapy

☐ Consistent nutrition

☐ Regular exercise

☐ Regular meditation, or some sort of relaxation or spirituality practice

☐ Regular fun activities: movie nights, date nights, trips to a theme park or the beach/cabin/lake/state park, cooking classes, etc.

For the Family

☐ Regular attendance at Al-Anon meetings

☐ Regular individual therapy for each family member

☐ Regular couples or family therapy

☐ Consistent nutrition

☐ Regular exercise

☐ Regular meditation, or some sort of relaxation or spirituality practice

☐ Regular fun activities: movie nights, date nights, trips to a theme park or the beach/cabin/lake/state park, cooking classes, etc.

chapter nine

RESOURCES TO CONTINUE YOUR JOURNEY

Chapter 9

Resources to Continue Your Journey

O nce you and your family have completed Plan A or Plan B, one of the best things that you can do is have an ongoing commitment to follow-through. What does follow-through mean? Ongoing individual and family therapy among you, your family, and your loved one to continue working through the reasons the addict in your family may have used. This ongoing therapy can also mean introducing both your loved one and each member of the family to a group of supportive individuals who can understand the struggle of staying clean.

For hundreds of thousands of addicts throughout the country, support groups provide a place to be honest, to feel welcomed, to talk about their difficulties without judgment, and to find others who have been or currently are going through the same experiences.

A number of options and resources are available for both you and your family member. You can spend some time on the internet, researching each option, and from there, decide which ones may be best for you and your loved one. Additionally, ask your family member what they would find the most helpful and be most comfortable with using will help you narrow down your choices and find the right fit. The best thing I can recommend is that you go to meetings, meet the therapists, read books, watch videos and engage in the recovery communities and see where you fit in. The internet is great for making lists and getting directions but I have worked with too many people who look at a website and find some small trivial reason that keeps them from actually participating or going to an event and getting involved. There is no substitute for direct human contact with other people fighting the same battle as you.

Ask your therapist and your loved one's therapist about groups recommended for people who have found themselves in your situation. Your therapist will likely have significant knowledge of the best support groups in your area for your particular situation and can give you recommendations based on their experience with you and your family. Many groups will have several day and time choices for meetings, so you can also try out a few different groups in your area to find one that will provide you and your loved with the most support. If you cannot find anything in your area, contact us and we will help you find some.

Resources for You and Your Family

Al-Anon www.alanon.org

Al-Anon may be one of the most recognized and widely used support group services in the country. The website has an FAQ section that you can browse if you are not sure what you are looking for or what going to a meeting may look like. Al-Anon is not for alcoholics; it is designed as a support system for those who are in the same situation that you find yourself in: they are the family and friends of alcoholics. The focus of Al-Anon rests on helping to deal with and solve the most common problems that families of those with an addiction to alcohol often face.

It is important to note that at Al-Anon meetings, the alcoholic is generally not included. It can be easier for the families of alcoholics to speak freely about their experiences without the addict there, so they will have separate meetings and support groups of their own.

Al-Anon is for the family of an alcoholic, not an addict or alcoholic, specifically. Please also note that the primary individuals who attend Al-Anon meetings are those who have a family member or friend who is an alcoholic, not a drug addict. If your child's problem revolves around drug use, you may find Nar-Anon more helpful.

Nar-Anon www.nar-anon.org

Nar-Anon, like Al-Anon, consists of group meetings for the families and friends of addicts. The Nar-Anon program consists of twelve steps, like NA or AA, and bases its program off of those. Again, like any of the other "Anonymous" meetings, there are no fees to pay or rules for joining; you and your family simply attend a group in order to participate. If your child has had a drug problem, Nar-Anon may be your best bet to find support in your community. The website will have lists of meeting times and places in your area, you can look for the organization in the white pages, or you can simply search online to find a meeting close by. If there is no Nar-Anon group in your area, the website will allow you to click through a link to start one.

Adult Children of Alcoholics (ACA) www.adultchildren.org

If you have older kids or teens who have been affected by drinking in your family, this is a great resource for them. Often, parents may figure out, through their struggle with their child who uses drugs or abuses alcohol, that they may have a problem, themselves, or that they may be the child of an alcoholic and have not been aware of it until now.

ACA can be a tremendous resource for individuals who find themselves in this situation. As adults, many people process the events of their childhood differently than they would if they were kids, and they can also learn to recognize behaviors that they engage in because their parents were alcoholics and they may not have known it. Additionally, growing up in an alcoholic household can do lasting damage to relationships with others, and part of the healing process can be working through those issues in a safe and supportive environment. If this sounds familiar to you, ACA may be a good choice. Once again, visit their website for meeting times and places in your area, or learn how to start one yourself.

SMART Recovery https://www.smartrecovery.org

Families Anonymous https://www.familiesanonymous.org

Resources for Your Loved One

Having covered a few of the best resources for you and your family while you go through the hard work of moving forward from your family member's alcoholism or drug addiction, now it's time to go over a few of the things your loved one may find the most helpful. These resources will be particularly helpful if your family member has spent time in a rehabilitation or treatment center, or lived in a group home or halfway house, as many times those environments implement many of the techniques used in these resources.

Alcoholics Anonymous (AA) www.aa.org

Probably the most well-known resource worldwide for those who struggle with alcohol addiction and dependence, AA is the most likely place for your loved one to start if they have had a drinking problem. AA meetings are often widely attended and can have specific markers for attendance, such as meetings for men, meetings for women, and meetings for teenagers. There are usually several meetings a day in most metropolitan areas, and they are held at a variety of locations.

AA will provide your loved one with a support system of individuals who have faced or are facing an addiction to alcohol. Your family member simply has to attend to take part, and there are no fees or charges. At a meeting, your loved one will meet a sponsor, someone to whom they can talk if they are feeling the urge to drink or even just having a hard time. The program is run based on the twelve-step system. Many people attend AA meetings for most or all of their lives, even if they are not currently drinking, because of the support the meetings can provide on the road to and during sobriety.

Narcotics Anonymous (NA) www.na.org

NA, like AA, is a widely used resource for those struggling with addiction and it has become more frequent over recent years, due to the increasing availability of narcotics and the uptick in users all over the country. Like AA, there are many options for meetings, and you will likely find one in your area that will meet the needs of your family member the best. The foundations of NA are also similar and use the twelve-step system to work through the addict's issues. NA is a program that requires complete abstinence from all drugs, so it is important that your family member understands that they cannot attend these meetings if they are using at all.

Cocaine Anonymous (CA) www.ca.org

Another option in the twelve-step recovery system is Cocaine Anonymous (CA), so if your loved one's drug problem has revolved around cocaine or any other drugs, you may want to send them to these meetings, instead of AA or NA.

SMART Recovery www.smartrecovery.org

SMART Recovery is an alternative to NA or AA, for those who do not find these programs helpful. SMART Recovery is a four-point program that utilizes a science-based system to help your family member maintain sobriety. The program avoids the use of words such as "addict" or "alcoholic", so if you find that your child struggles with these particular labels, this may be an option for them. SMART is based around the idea that using alcohol and drugs is a way to cope with problems and emotional upsets but can become problematic when drinking or drug use become heavy or out of control. The SMART program focuses on research-based techniques to help your loved one work through their daily life after they are sober and learn to deal with problems that they may face as they arise.

Generally speaking, SMART Recovery does not focus on past experiences as much as NA or AA does. If your loved one finds that that

-224-

setup does not work for them, they may want to give SMART a try. There are no sponsors in SMART Recovery; instead, the meetings are run by facilitators, some of whom are professionals or who have had issues with drugs or alcohol in the past, some of whom have not. While the program at SMART Recovery meetings differs from that of NA or AA meetings, many individuals attend both and can find both helpful for different reasons. While SMART is not a spin-off of the "Anonymous" program, the two can be used concurrently if your loved one finds that they are helpful.

Also note that SMART Recovery offers meetings and programs for friends and families of addicts and alcoholics, as well as ones that are based around any court-ordered support group participation, and they also have meetings designed specifically for teenagers and younger people.

Celebrate Recovery www.celebraterecovery.com

Celebrate Recovery is similar to NA and AA in that it utilizes a twelve-step program, but their program is specifically designed around faith. If you or your family member is religious, then Celebrate Recovery may be a good choice for you, particularly if your loved one has found support at church, or if their faith helps them to stay clean or sober. They use Step Studies, The Journey Begins, and The Journey Continues to denote different levels of their program, and the CR program is open to anyone who has struggled with substance or alcohol abuse.

As you can see, there are quite a few options available for you, your family, and your loved one. Your best bet may be to try several of these options to find the one that works the best and is in line with the way that you want to handle your family member's substance abuse and the way that they see themselves moving forward in recovery. If finances are a problem, the free meetings are a wonderful option for finding support and hope, without having to pay for something that you or your family cannot afford.

Remember that this is a limited list, and there may be more available options for you. Ask your therapist what they would recommend and spend some time searching the internet for options in your area. You may want to begin doing this research immediately upon realizing that your loved one has a problem; whether you use Plan A, Plan B, or both, ideally, you do not want there to be a gap in your loved one's recovery. Having meetings or programs picked out and ready to attend will help your family member stay clean and stay sober from the first day forward.

KEY TAKEAWAYS:

- An ongoing commitment to follow-through is critical for your journey.

- Finding the best option may be a matter of trying several options to find the one that works the best and is in line with the way that you want to handle your loved one's substance abuse and healing the family.

- Just because your family member is sober now does not mean the problem is solved. Everyone needs to take care of themselves in order to be present in the family.

- There are a ton of options for individual and family recovery; try them out and see which one works for you.

- The best way you can support your loved one's recovery is to get serious about your own recovery and mental health. Remember, you cannot expect your family member to do something you are not willing to do.

Chapter 9: Worksheet

Keep track of the meetings you plan to attend with a paper calendar or an app on your phone. For each meeting, be sure to note the time and location. When you've attended 90 meetings, reward yourself!

Sunday	Monday	Tuesday	Wednesday	Thursday	Friday	Saturday

chapter ten

ONE YEAR LATER

Chapter 10

One Year Later

Your loved one came home from a rehab facility with a treatment plan. Your job, as the spouse, parent, or sibling of a person in recovery is to follow the treatment plan for the family. The focus in the days, weeks, months, and years after your family member's recovery is on *you*, not on them. As you read in Chapter 8, plan on attending regular meetings, regularly. Go to individual therapy as well as couples therapy or family therapy. Then, be sure you are eating well, exercising, meditating, and having fun with your family. Finally, read the books I suggest and stay engaged.

One of my main challenges as a licensed marriage and family therapist is getting people to learn how to take care of *themselves* and not be focused on their loved one. That's the big issue: for so long, you've been constantly focused on the individual in your family who has struggled with an addition. But now, it's time for you to focus on yourself. If you've started to see the signs of codependency in yourself, continue to work on that.

Here's an overview of several family issues that you may find helpful to review as you navigate the months and years ahead:

1. **What is codependency?** Codependency is driven by the agreement that I will work harder on your problem and your life than you do and I will blame you for not listening to me or taking more initiative. It often sounds like this: "After all I have done for you, this is how you repay me!"

2. **What is enabling?** Rescuing someone who continues to make poor choices is not called love, it's called enabling. Stop enabling and refuse to be a safety net, so they can grow up. Enabling often sounds like this: "If I don't do it for them, then it will not happen." Remember, "Help is the sunny side of control."

3. **What is people-pleasing?** It's fine to want to please someone you care about, but codependents usually don't think they have a choice. Saying "No" causes them anxiety. Some codependents have a hard time saying "No" to anyone. They go out of their way and sacrifice their own needs to accommodate other people. People pleasing often sounds like this: "I just want everyone to get along and not fight, even if it means sacrificing my needs."

4. **What does passive-aggressive mean?** Conflict avoidant and sabotaging instead of standing up for yourself and saying what you think or want. People with passive-aggressive behavior express their negative feelings subtly through their actions instead of handling them directly. This creates a separation between what they say and what they do. For example, say someone proposes a plan at work. A person with passive-aggressive behavior may oppose the plan, but instead of voicing their opinion, they say that they agree with it. Since they're actually against the plan, however, they resist following it. They may purposely miss deadlines, turn up late to meetings, and undermine the plan in other ways.

5. **What is caretaking?** If someone else has a problem, you want to help them to the point that you give up yourself. It's natural to feel empathy and sympathy for someone, but codependents start putting other

people ahead of themselves. In fact, they *need* to help and might feel rejected if another person doesn't want help. Moreover, they keep trying to help and fix the other person, even when that person clearly isn't taking their advice.

6. **What is denial?** Codependents deny their feelings and needs. Often, they don't know what they're feeling and are instead focused on what others are feeling. The same thing goes for their needs. They pay attention to other people's needs and not their own. They might be in denial of their need for space and autonomy. Although some codependents seem needy, others act like they're self-sufficient when it comes to needing help. They won't reach out and have trouble receiving.

7. **Isn't everybody who is a parent codependent?** Probably. As our kids get older, we have to let go and allow them to learn their life lessons on their own. Sometimes that means watching them run into a wall at full speed. Ask yourself, "How many times have I told them not to do that and yet they still do it?" Kids have to learn from their own experiences, or the lessons don't stick with them.

8. **How do we stop being codependent?** Educate yourself by reading *Codependent No More, Facing Codependency,* and *Unspoken Legacy.* Find a therapist in your area that you can meet with who understands

codependency and how it works. Go to AlAnon, CODA, NarAnon, meetings regularly and work the steps with a sponsor. Attend a weekly family support meeting.

9. **Why do we have to go to meetings?** Because addiction affects the whole family, not just the addict. The entire family system has to change in order to not repeat the past. Remember, "You're not responsible for your family member's addiction but you are responsible for how you react to it," and, "You cannot expect the addict in the family to do something that you are not willing to do yourself."

Quite honestly, the year after the loved one comes home from treatment is where families drop the ball. This is why it's just so critical to repeat myself here. I'll tell you a story to further illustrate: I was seeing a 17-year-old boy, a kid who was talented enough at his sport to play at the Division One level in college. So, his parents decided to pull them out of treatment for a weekend because he had to go to some tournament in a different state. They told me, "It is just critical that he go, you understand…if he doesn't, it's going to affect his chances of getting into a top division one school…" Blah blah blah.

They were all over the place. They were scattered, and they were not reading the books, they did not have a plan as a family. When it was time for this teen to come home from treatment, they were panicking and freaking out. It was a mess. Let me be clear with you: when you don't follow through, or when you put things ahead of your loved one's sobriety, there is trouble.

Three things can happen when the loved one comes home from treatment:

1. The families get fully on board. They completely dig in, start taking care of themselves, pursue their own recovery, and do exactly what I tell them to do. When this is the case, the transitions are almost seamless. They're fantastic and they're straightforward, and the chances of a relapse is lessened.

2. Next, we get the families that are partially on board. They will do the reading, the family therapy, and some of the engagement with the treatment program. But they aren't going to the 12-step meetings. In this situation, things are actually okay. They're not great, but they're okay.

3. Third, there are families that won't do anything. They give it a lot of lip service and then they start looking for better, easier options. Things go all over the place; it is total insanity and total crisis. Families like this see their loved one cycle back into treatment because the family

hasn't changed. We bring the kid or the adult home and there's no support. People aren't being self-aware and taking care of their own business. It's still this dynamic of: "*You're* the problem, and if it wasn't for *you*, then we wouldn't have to do any of this."

This is your chance to make a decision: which family will you be? In the year after your loved one comes home from treatment, I want to see the three things I mentioned earlier:

- Consistency: It creates success through repetition and conquers our old way of life.
- Accountability: It develops a sense of connection and community to help heal and keep egos in check. It also creates vulnerability with a sponsor, mentor, or a therapist.
- Transparency: This means having everything on the table with nothing hidden in the closet.

All of these items are easier to create when the members of your family are meeting regularly, asking questions, and starting to have awareness of themselves, as in, "Oh, *that's* what you were talking about." I had a chat yesterday with a woman whose son went to treatment; now he's in extended care. It's been a little bit of a battle to get her to go to

Codependents Anonymous but now she is going. And she said, "I'm starting to see things in a new way."

The idea is to have a revelation: "Oh, I get it. All those things you were talking about? The list of codependent traits? I'm starting to see those things in me." Our conversations tend to be about the person sitting in front of me, not about their loved one who has just come out of treatment.

It's okay to call for a tune-up

You can do a check-in with a family therapist six months, a year, two years later. Say, "We've got a little bit of *this* going on, a little bit of *that* going on." Generally, what I do is I run through the checklist with them: What's the after-treatment plan for the individual and for the family? Are you doing therapy? Are you doing family therapy? Are you following through regarding your self-care? Nutrition, exercise, meditation, having fun?

When I hear, "We're too busy," I remind families that *when nothing changes, nothing changes.* So, it's really about being able to walk through that checklist and say, "Here's the deal, the families who are successful are in it." They're in the 12-step programs. The people that actually go to meetings, get a sponsor, and work the steps both for addiction and for codependency get better, and they stay better.

The people who are too busy, who say things like, "Well, I've got to take care of this other thing, I can't spend all my time on this," will suffer. Remember, I'm a consultant. The house is on fire? The business is failing? You've brought me in to assess the business, I've given you my assessment, and your answer is, "We're not going to do that. What else do you have?" My answer always is, "This is it; I'm a one trick pony. You follow the plan, your life gets better. If you don't follow the plan your life does not. It's that simple."

Family recovery in real life

I want you to hear from one of my clients who has done tremendous work. Reading her experience here will give you a solid idea of what progress looks like when families and individuals dig in and change at the same time their loved one changes. She'll stay anonymous, of course, but I think you'll understand as you read why I wanted her to share her story in this chapter:

"My parents divorced when I was quite young. My dad's an alcoholic; my mom's a classic narcissist. My brother got into drugs early.

He passed away a couple years ago from an overdose. I had a second brother and stepbrother also. My mom remarried when I was in my teens and that brother died of drugs as well. So, addiction was part of my family history.

"Then I married and had three kids, and my middle boy started struggling with marijuana when he was in high school. He ended up dropping out. He's now had his one-year sobriety. My son's been in treatment on and off for quite a while, and when he was at Jay Walker in Colorado, they put me in touch with Kevin. I resisted doing my own treatment until fairly recently, but I have gotten into my own treatment since then, and it's changed my behavior to the point where my recovering son just came home for a week and said it was like superhuman how completely different my parenting is now.

"I consider myself a fairly smart and high functioning person. Everybody in my family is extremely high functioning. My parents, my husband, my children, everybody…they're just really high functioning and I carry with me the concept of from my childhood that it's not okay to not deliver. And so, when my middle son was in his treatment, and I started working with Kevin, I was in this fog of, 'It's not my problem. It's his problem, why should I have to change my life when he's the one who's screwing everything up?' I guess I sort of thought I was too squared away to really need my own treatment and it took me a while to find the right groups.

"I have the attitude, *if there's a problem, fix it.* I don't like talking about problems. I don't like people who talk about problems and don't do anything about them. And so, I went through several different programs. I'd go to one meeting and there'd be a handful of people who would talk about the same problem over and over and over again. And I'd say, *this is not for me.* Kevin just sort of hung in there with me and said, 'Okay, well, read this. Read that.' I was great at reading information. Finally, I got into the right group. It was almost like my son wasn't in crisis anymore, so I felt like I had the bandwidth to focus on what I had considered to be superfluous stuff. It was like, 'Okay, now I'll focus on my stuff.' I started realizing how intricately intertwined my issues were with my son's recovery.

"The analogy that I have is that we all have our own house and we all have our own stuff that we carry with us when we leave our house. From the time I was a child, I was taught that it was my job to carry everybody's stuff all the time. I was the perfect child. I was the savior. I was the one who was taking care of my brother and his drugs, taking care of my mom and her exhaustion. I carried everybody's shit all the time. When my son got into recovery, I was carrying all his stuff, too. But I didn't want to put it down because it was my job.

"Finally, Kevin and my group helped me figure out that I had to open my own suitcases and start cleaning them out. You know, put my stuff away in my house. I still *had* this stuff but I knew where it was and I knew how to handle it. I knew how to keep it organized, yet it wasn't in my suitcase anymore. I didn't have to carry it around with me. Only then could I realize that I was still carrying my kids' suitcases around with me. But it was *their* job. I couldn't empty their suitcases for them. I had to give their suitcases back to them and tell them to take it into their own house and empty it out and organize it in the ways that made sense to them. I couldn't see that until I started emptying out my own suitcase.

"I couldn't even put their stuff *down* until I started looking at my own stuff. Again, it wasn't that you were getting rid of the stuff in your suitcase. You just organized it. It's all part of who you are, it's all part of your house. But you can put it away someplace where it's safe. Then you walk out on the street and you don't even have a suitcase anymore. You just have a little handbag. You meet up with your kid and he doesn't have his suitcases anymore. He just has a little handbag, too. And you've gotten this clean, effective interaction that you just never had before.

"It was really interesting because my husband is sort of head down in his job, as in, 'Oh honey, you're so confident. I know you can handle all this, you have so much of a better relationship with the kids than I do.' When our son was home, my husband said to us, 'How do you know what to do? This is working so much better.' My son said to my husband, 'Dad, Mom's done all this work, and she's totally different. You've done nothing and it hurts me that you don't care enough to have done any work.' The programs my son has been in have been very good at giving him a voice. I don't know whether my husband's communicated with Kevin or not. That's his stuff that he needs to do. But it's definitely changed enough that my husband feels like he wants to be part of the change.

"If you trust your kids to survive making bad choices, it gives them the ability to move forward and not be scared of making bad choices. But it was always my job, when I was young, to protect everybody from their bad choices. Until I started doing this work, I was carrying that with me into adulthood. My mom and I are very close and I recognize all of her downfalls. I was fortunate enough that she married a man who also recognizes her downfalls and who has slowly, given me books about growing up with a narcissistic parent. He's such an amazing man. He started giving me permission to recognize who my mom is. I accept her and love her and adore her but understand where we all have our shortcomings.

"If you can detach yourself from somebody else's baggage and just focus on your own stuff, like me with my parents, then that leads you to be able to also do it with your own family, as I did with my children. A year later, it's just no more chaos. When you are codependent in an addiction, it makes you crazy. It genuinely makes you crazy. There's this weight that gets lifted off of you when something clicks into place. You realize that that's not yours to carry. My child is doing this hell of a job, dealing with his issues. And the best way for me to help with that is not to get involved in his process, but to do my own process so that when he steps into this new independent adult life, where he where he's dealing with his issues—without that really intense recovery support—that I don't add to the issues, I just support him in his recovery. It's very liberating to disentangle yourself from passive addiction. The smoke clears. The smoke is not blowing out of his addiction and into mine. And my codependence is blowing away.

"As a high functioning adult, you're like, 'Okay, I may have stuff, but it's not really relevant.' What I mean is I have these two other kids. My oldest son is an Ivy League graduate who works in New York as a consultant. He's super successful. And my youngest son is probably the sweetest human being you'll ever meet. He's very good, highly functional, blah blah blah. And my middle son, unfortunately for him, he's got a lot of the genetic markers that my brother also carried, an addictive personality. As a parent with these, these wildly different children, you can look at the two that are functioning and say, 'Well, it's not my fault because I've got these two kids who are great. But now that I started looking into my own stuff, I see where I need to really give them permission to be more their own person and make their own mistakes. It's hard when you have that *it's not my fault* approach. I mean, it's not a 'fault' thing, it's just that we all need to alter the way we do things a little bit.

"What was so genius about Kevin, and I wish every human being in my position could have a Kevin, is that he doesn't 'therapy' you. He comes to where you are and he's like, 'okay, that's where you are. You need to keep considering these things but I'll just hang out with you until you're ready to move to a different place. He's just wonderful."

Year One

The first year of sobriety, in my experience, is just about staying sober. It's about keeping your head above water. I was 27 that year and at my first office job, my first real job. I was going to college sober, I was dating sober, and it felt like there were all these rules. I had worked in restaurants where it was just fly-by-night in terms of acceptable behavior. But of course, that crap doesn't get very far in an office. For example, I got in trouble one time for eating off of somebody else's plate. I stole a fry from somebody. The people that I had worked in restaurants with would never have cared. But in an office environment, somebody felt really offended. That was my first introduction to people getting wound up about protocol. It was very eye-opening.

The first year is just the addict asking, "How do I not drink? How do I not use drugs? And how do I show up and be present?" My head was spinning that first year.

Year One Through Year Five

The first five years is really about learning how to live sober. It's gathering the life skills you need to survive: How do you get a real job? How do you pay your bills? Year two to year five, it's like, "Okay, I can do this." Then, "How do I date properly? How do I manage money?" I remember when I used to pay my bills in those early years, it felt like such an accomplishment. Back in the day, we wrote a check and stuck it in the mailbox. I would expect trumpets to sound when I completed this task!

In AA, we call it the Holy Trinity: get a girlfriend, get a job, get a car. When someone in recovery gets these things, they generally disappear from the meetings. I'm not saying you have to go every day to maintain your sobriety, but you do have to actively work at it. Let's use the analogy of going to the gym. You want to have a good body? You want to be in good shape? You've got to exercise regularly. Not once a week. Not twice a week. Regularly. And as you know, in the gym or anything else, there's a culture that goes with it. You need to buy into the culture. The same thing works for recovery with addiction and codependency. It's not just going to the meetings, there's the culture you've got to buy into.

Keep showing up and participating and being engaged. I would say the markers after that are like eight to 10 and then like 15 to 20. You've got to get deeper; you've got to go down further, you've got to dig in, and get to the really good stuff. You'll start to see the issues in your life and where they come from.

People start finding when they get into relationships, that they have to learn how to *behave* in relationships because alcoholics and addicts, all we know how to do is go to a bar and hook up. But we don't know how to date. We don't know how to behave. Codependents are the same: all they know how to do is reach out and grab onto people and hold on to them and force them into a certain way of life. So, it's really about embracing the culture and embracing the life skills. The further in you get, the deeper you go. For me, it's been about addressing my family of origin issues. When you do that, you're like, "Yeah. Now I get it." That's really the challenge now.

You know, right now, the country feels like it's been traumatized. Everybody's just freaking out. Yet everybody shows up at my doorstep and says, "No, there's no history of mental health or substance abuse issues in my family, ever." And I'm like, "Okay cool. I know you believe that. That's cute."

Growing up in an alcoholic home, in which mom and dad are constantly fighting reminds me of this moment in our country, in which the two political parties are fighting. What happens when mom and dad are locked into Mortal Kombat is that the kids naturally start forming certain behavior patterns and going into certain what we call archetypes.

You have the fighter, who is so angry and so frustrated. He's just going to pick a fight and go nuts because that's how he expresses himself. Next, you have the addict who will find something to soothe their soul. It's going to be drugs, it's going to be alcohol, it's going to be food it's going to be gambling, it's going to be sex, it's going to be porn. Then you have the perfect child who is going to make sure everything's okay and make sure everybody's happy and make sure everything looks right and everything's nice, thinking, "If I get straight A's, people will be happy." Then you have the ostrich who sticks his head in the sand and is like, "I don't know. There's no addiction, there's no drugs or alcoholism, there's no fighting, nobody's getting beaten up, there's no broken doors. I don't know what you're talking about." Finally, you have the caretaker who's going to spend all their time nurturing everybody else, because mom and dad aren't.

Meanwhile, mom and dad are going to war. Right now, due to Covid-19, we have body counts on the news and it's terrifying. It's so traumatizing for everyone, so it helps to have a big systemic understanding of this. Just as kids react in a house of addiction, all those ways I just mentioned are how people are reacting to this moment in history. We need leaders to step up to the plate and say, "I got you. We are going to make sure everyone is okay."

The two forces, mom and dad, or the two political parties, are angry and fighting—going after each other's throats. While that's happening, the kids are not being tended to. The country is not being nurtured. That's the great tragedy. When someone struggles with addiction in the house, you have to take care of the whole family, not just the individual.

When is this over?

Because this chapter is about one year later, two years later, and beyond, you might be wondering, "At what point is this over?" When you look at the spectrum of care, starting with detox, where your loved one is in the hospital for three to 10 days, and you roll all the way over to just going into outpatient therapy, and meetings, the cost is dwindling tremendously. Let's say the addict is sober and has been sober for a year. The care they need and the cost of that care will be very manageable.

The whole point is that in the initial part of this journey, you need a lot of focus and attention to change things, and then you can slowly move it down to just doing maintenance level work. Meetings are free, or they're a dollar. It's like when you have surgery. You've got to go to physical therapy three times a week, then it's two times a week, then it's one time a week. Then, you don't need physical therapy. Instead, you go to the gym and immerse yourself in a culture of health. You have to change the system, change the behavior, and change the way you live.

Otherwise, you'll have to go get surgery again. If a diabetic goes off sugar for the next six years and then a year and a half later, they're coming back with high numbers and having struggles, it's probably because their diet changed. It's not rocket science. It needs to be really clear:

- Go to meetings
- Get a sponsor
- Work the steps
- Your life will change

Go to couple's therapy, and things will get better, but you must go with an intent to change, not just for the hell of it. For example, your spouse may have gone to treatment for 30 days, and now she is home. So, it's time to talk about what's been going on for the last ten years.

We're going to talk about things like, why did you tolerate this for so long? Everything's a two-way street. I get a lot of people that come out of individual treatment, and are told to call me for a couple's therapy. What the spouse wants is an opportunity to beat up on the person who's in recovery. And I'm like, "No, we're not doing that. Happy couples and happy families come from happy individuals. Happy individuals work on their stuff."

Final Thoughts

There isn't going to be a moment where you say, "That's it! We're done! Everything is perfect." Addiction and codependency aren't like that. That's now how this works. It's not as if you're magically all better and you never have to deal with these issues again. *I wish.* Wouldn't that be great?

One of things you have to understand is that if you're an alcoholic or an addict, six months later, you can't start drinking again. Do you know what the relapse rates are for people who go to treatment? They're so high (between 40% and 60%, according to drugabuse.gov). Because the families are like, "Oh yeah, he went to treatment and it's okay, he only drinks once in a while now." When I hear this, I know the family system didn't change. Sometimes I hear a person who was an opiate addict claim it is okay for them to drink. No. That's BS. If I'm addicted to drugs and alcohol, that's it. When you're in recovery, it's not a cafeteria where you can pick and choose. And yes, you can be addicted to marijuana.

You have to get past the idea that being in recovery—or having a family member in recovery—is some sort of death sentence or scar. It's not. It's the best thing. I love AA; I love the people. It's what has created my life and what got me to where I am today. It's brought me relationships, a whole career, and fulfillment as a human being.

I am living the life that I want to live, doing what I want to do, with the people I want to be doing it with. I am engaged in this. It's exciting, it's awesome, and it never would've happened if I hadn't been an alcoholic who went to AA.

Remember, recovery is a journey for the entire family. Use consistency, accountability, and transparency for all family members. Continue with individual and family therapy, 12-Step meetings, and faith-based community support groups. You can do it.

Chart your family's progress on this Spectrum of Care:

1 **Medical Detox Facility**
3–7 Days

2 **Residential Treatment Center (RTC)**
14-28 Days

3 **Partial Hospitilization Program (PHP)**
6-12 Weeks

4 **Intensive Outpatient Program (IOP)**
6-12 Weeks

5 **Sober Living Home**
3–12 Months

Family Checklist

Have things changed?

_____

_____

Are you maintaining your health and sobriety?

_____

_____

Are you going to meetings?

_____

_____

Is the relationship better?

_____

_____

How's your mental, physical, and emotional health?

_____

_____

How are grades? Work?

_____

_____

Appendix 1

12-Step-based Recovery Programs

Alcoholics Anonymous www.aa.org

Cocaine Anonymous https://www.ca.org

Drug Addicts Anonymous https://www.daausa.org

Al-Anon Family Groups www.al-anon.org

Adult Children of Alcoholics https://adultchildren.org

Codependents Anonymous http://coda.org

Families Anonymous https://www.familiesanonymous.org

Appendix 2

Governing Bodies and Associations for Treatment Programs and Professionals

National Association of Addiction Treatment Providers
https://www.naatp.org

The Independent Educational Consultants Association (IECA)
https://www.iecaonline.com

National Association of Therapeutic Schools and Programs
https://natsap.org

Association of Intervention Specialists
associationofinterventionspecialists.org

NAADAC, Association for Addiction Professionals
https://www.naadac.org

Appendix 3

Dr. Kevin McCauley's 10 Principles

1. **90 Days of Residential Treatment.** It has been demonstrated that 30 and 60 days of treatment are insufficient to provide a solid foundation for recovery. A full 90 days in a residential program provides a strong base for ongoing recovery.

2. **Seamless Transition into a Sober Living Environment.** McCauley emphasizes that the addict should visit sober living houses — and choose the one he or she will move into — while still in residential treatment. Upon release from the inpatient facility, the recovering addict should be transported directly to the sober living environment

so there is no time during this vulnerable transition for the addict to obtain drugs or alcohol.

3. **Frequent, Non-Random Drug Testing.** Drug testing must continue throughout the first year of recovery and be performed at frequent enough intervals to detect any time the addict uses his or her drug of choice. Any lower frequency gives the addict a window in which to use with impunity, which is a disservice to the recovering addict: a clean test enhances motivation for recovery.

4. **Outpatient Treatment Program.** While the addict is residing at a sober living environment after being released from residential care, he or she needs to continue treatment. This will entail working with a drug addiction counselor and may include individual, family and/or group therapy.

5. **A Relapse Prevention Plan.** A recovering addict may be exposed to old triggers to drink or use, and new situations are likely to arise in which he or she will have impulses to use again. Very early in outpatient treatment — if this has not been done during the residential stay — it is helpful for an addict, in the presence of his or her therapist, to draw up a relapse prevention plan that spells out in detail who to call, where to go and what to do when impulses to use arise. The addict

should write out his or her plan, carry it at all times, and use it religiously as needed.

6. **90 AA Meetings in 90 Days**. "90 in 90" means that the addict should attend at least 90 meetings in his first 90 days of being in outpatient treatment. This gives the recovering addict a firm footing in the recovery community of Alcoholics Anonymous. In the environment of AA, the recovering addict can learn sober ways of thinking, behaving and coping, and observe sober people who are creating sober lives for themselves. AA offers the addict a community in which to develop personal connections and to feel a sense of belonging.

7. **Meeting with an Addiction Physician**. There can be medical complications resulting from addiction, and a physician versed in the physical effects of addiction, and the physical changes that accompany recovery, will be best able to help the addict understand and manage his symptoms.

8. **Meeting with an Addiction Psychiatrist**. There may be psychiatric issues that preceded addiction or that arose during the period of use, and a psychiatrist who is knowledgeable about the psychological issues that accompany drug and alcohol dependence can distinguish psychological symptoms that are transitory aspects of recovery from those that may benefit from psychotropic medication. Sometimes an

addict needs a period of time to be sober before a psychiatrist can determine what symptoms are likely to clear up with sobriety.

9. **Return to Work.** Returning to work is an important aspect of becoming a fully functional after a lapse into addiction. Furthermore, work helps build self-esteem and offset the shame that generally accompanies addiction and job loss. Someone in early recovery may benefit from choosing a lower-stress job than he or she had previously, since the goal of working at this phase of recovery is to provide consistency, structure, responsibility and an opportunity to perform well rather than to embark on, or resume, a particular career path. For some people in recovery, return to a previous job is appropriate, but for others this is not the case. Determining what constitutes appropriate work for a specific individual is a topic that the recovering addict can person discuss with a therapist or group leader.

10. **Fun.** The dopamine that has been depleted in addiction needs replenishment. Learning non-drug-using ways to produce pleasure is essential to rebuilding the natural supplies of dopamine. Without dopamine, recovery will not be appealing; the addict will experience more pain than pleasure, and the option of returning to alcohol or drugs in order to feel good will be compelling.

Following these ten principles can be a tall order, which is why the person in recovery, and his or her family, can benefit from substantial support and guidance. A counselor can reinforce these principles, and can steer the recovering person to their close adherence, for the sake of building a solid recovery platform.

Appendix 4

Reach the Experts

Holly Wilson, MA, LPCC

> 3801 E Florida Ave, Ste 650
>
> Denver, CO 80210
>
> www.womensrecovery.com
>
> (888) 233-1553
>
> info@womensrecovery.com
>
> **Instagram:** instagram.com/womens.recovery/
>
> **Facebook:** facebook.com/womensrecovery1/
>
> **Twitter:** twitter.com/WomensRecovery2

Nikki Soda

Membership Development Officer

1120 Lincoln Street, Suite 1104

Denver, CO 80203

nsoda@naatp.org

303.550.9982 | naatp.org

Charles Van Leuven, NCRC ll, NCLAMA

National Treatment Transport

www.safetransport.com

1-833-680-SAFE (7233)

Mobile (415) 225-0137

Charlie@safetransport.com

Keith Bradley

Founder/Interventionist

Love in Action Interventions and Training

(970) 381-9780

Keith@coloradointervention.com

www.coloradointervention.com

Michael Barnes, PhD., MAC, LPC

    Chief Clinical Officer

    ForgingNewLives.com

    Phone: 844-955-1066

    Mobile: 303-885-1846

Brennon Moore, MS, CTT, CADC-II, LPC

    SkylineRecoveryBend.com

    BrennonPatrickMoore.com

    541-980-7542

    brennonpatrickmoore@gmail.com

The Phoenix

    ThePhoenix.org

    Founder: Scott Strode

    2239 Champa Street

    Denver, CO 80205

    720-440-9175

    info@thephoenix.org

Appendix 5

Recap

Plan A: Boundaries, accountability, rewards and consequences

Plan B: Treatment

Plan C: If your family member refuses to accept either Plan A or Plan B, they are no longer welcome to be in the family.

Appendix 6

Book List

Codependent No More by Melody Beattie

Chronic Hope: Parenting the Addicted Child by Kevin Petersen

Daring Greatly by Brené Brown (also watch her TED Talks from 2010 (Vulnerability) and 2012 (Shame) on vulnerability and shame. These will help you understand what your family member is experiencing.

Parenting Teens with Love and Logic, by Foster Kline, M.D., and Jim Fay

In the Realm of Hungry Ghosts, by Dr. Gabor Mate

Facing Codependence: What It Is, Where It Comes from, How It Sabotages Our Lives by Pia Mellody

Alcoholics Anonymous and Paths to Recovery

Appendix 7

The 12 Steps for Codependent Families

The 12 Steps as outlined by Alcoholics Anonymous are not just for the addicted person in your family. These steps can and should be used by everyone in your family to change the system and create something new—and better. For each step, the addiction in question is not to a substance per se, it's to a pattern of behavior: controlling and managing others. To move through the steps, the previous step or steps must first be completed.

1) *We admit we are powerless over our addiction (in this case, controlling and managing other people or enabling them) and that our lives have become unmanageable.*

   a. Powerless: Once I start, I can't stop. And I can't not start.

     i.   Physical allergy

       a) The phenomenon of craving: once I start, I cannot stop. I have watched these codependent families and how they behave, and they literally cannot stop themselves.

       b) When you are hit by a train, it's the engine that kills you, not the caboose; it's the first drink or first controlling action, not the tenth.

       c) Once I start using or trying to manage others, I cannot stop on my own.

  b. Unmanageability

     i.   *Mental Obsession

       a) "This time it's going to be different and here's why." This is the lie we tell ourselves.

       b) I trick myself into thinking I can control my codependent behaviors without helps.

       c) The bedevilments on p. 52 of the Big Book (having trouble with personal relationships, being unable to control "our emotional natures," falling "prey" to misery and depression, not being able to make a living, a feeling of uselessness, being full of fear,

unhappy and of no real help to other people)

c.   Spiritual Malady: I won't ask for help. My ego and pride are too

strong.

        a)   I need help from a higher power that is not

human if I am powerless and unmanageable.

        b)   Treatment can be a place where people tell me

what to do, because I can't make those

decisions for myself.

Again, you can't go to the second step in the 12 Steps until you

believe the first step. Are you powerless over your codependency? Can you

control the other people in your life? Can you manage them? Can you

manage your life?

2.   *We come to believe that a power greater than ourselves could restore us to sanity.*

The point of this step is: have you tried everything else on your own?

Have you tried all the doctors, all the specialists? Have you played all

of your cards? Do you have anything left?

a.   Is your higher power everything or nothing? There are no

percentages. If your higher power is in charge, you don't need to manage other people's lives. Don't use your faith to manipulate or control other people. The results are not in your hands.

 i. Do I need a spiritual solution? Have I tried all of the other tricks?

 ii. Am I convinced by Step One that I need spiritual help?

This step can and does work for people who are atheist. The higher power can be the Universe, nature, The Force, simply energy. It can be the spirit of the people in the room, as in, "God speaks to us through other people." It can be whatever you want, just not another person.

You cannot move onto three until you do step two. When I work with the families, I ask if they're still trying to run the show. I have a teen in treatment, for example, whose parents have decided they need to take him out of treatment so he can play in a lacrosse tournament. NO! That's not how it's done. The family is not convinced. They haven't moved through steps one and two.

3. *We make a decision to turn our will and our lives over to the care of our higher power as we understand our higher power.* This step is us admitting, "We can't figure this out."

   a. Am I willing to ask my higher power for help? Are you really ready?

Steps four through nine are what we call "the work."

4. *We make a searching and fearless moral inventory.* I teach families to do this step (see the worksheet for this chapter) as this is what the addict will be doing in treatment. The point of this exercise is that we all walk around with this stuff and engaging in this inventory is how to get it out. Answer the following questions for yourself in a notebook and have each member of the family do so on their own. Get it all out on paper and share it with someone. The sponsor's job is to normalize behaviors and emotions. We need to dispel shame. One of the biggest reasons people don't want to go to meetings is they think, "I'm not like those people." Yes, you are. "I don't need this." To that, I say, "You need it double."

   Resentments: Who or what we are mad at? Please don't say, "I'm not angry." Everyone gets angry sometimes, and living with an addict isn't easy.

a. Who am I angry at?

b. What did they do to harm me?

c. (Okay to be the Victim) How does this affect:

    i. Ambition: what I want?

    ii. Self-Esteem: how I see myself?

    iii. Security: what makes me feel safe?

    iv. Pride: "I deserve..."

    v. Personal: "My friends/family think..."

    vi. Sex: The opposite sex will think...

    vii. Pocket Book: Money, time and effort

d. Looking at yourself:

    i. Selfish: Where am I being selfish in this process?

    ii. Dishonest: What lies am I telling myself and/or others?

    iii. Self-Seeking: What action do I take to force my will on others?

    iv. Afraid: What is my bottom-line fear?

Fear: What am I really afraid of here? Write down every fear I have:

a. Describe fear

    i. I'm afraid of elevators.

b. What's going to happen:

      i.   I'm afraid the cable will snap and I'll die.

  c. Selfishly try to protect and preserve my life by:

      i.   I avoid buildings that have elevators and only go to buildings with one floor.

  d. I am not trusting and relying on my higher power to care and protect me.

      i.   Point: We give our will over to my higher power, except in X situation. I'm not relying upon my higher power in X situation.

Conduct Inventory: Think of someone you've been in relationship with.

      i.   Selfish, dishonest, inconsiderate

     ii. Where have I been selfish, dishonest, and inconsiderate with them?

    iii. How have I hurt them?

    iv. Did I arouse jealousy, suspicion, or bitterness?

     v. Where was I at fault?

    vi. What should I have done instead?

5. *We admit to our higher power, to ourselves and to another human being the exact nature of our wrongs.*

a. Share this with a sponsor or a trusted advisor.

b. The sponsor then points out patterns and gives us a list of our defects of character.

6. *We are entirely ready to have our higher power remove all these defects of character.*

a. The patterns you and your sponsor saw when doing your fifth step.

7. *We humbly ask our higher power to remove our shortcomings.* This is important: our shortcomings don't magically go away. It's about acknowledging them, about creating an awareness. The idea is to continue to ask for help, and take these things to a therapist.

a. 7th step prayer.

b. How long did it take before your defects come back? How come?

c. When we rely on our higher power, that power begins to change these shortcomings, slowly and over time.

8. *We make a list of all persons we have harmed, and become willing to make amends to them all.*

a. Traditionally, we find the start of this list in our 4th step, for those we feel have wronged us, we tend to take action against.

b. What does "amends" mean? It's not an apology.

    i. "To fix," not to apologize.

9. *We make direct amends to such people whenever possible, except when to do so would injure them or others.*

a. Make an index card for each person you need to make amends to.

b. This process is not about putting myself in the other person's hands, but putting myself in my higher power's hands.

c. This is not a hang out, or spend time together afterwards.

    i. Here's the harm I caused you:

    ii. How did it affect you?

    iii. Any harms towards you I've left out?

    iv. How can I make it right?

The behavior change is so important here. You need to see that controlling and manipulating people is not the solution. The next three steps are sometimes referred to as the "maintenance steps."

10. *We continue to take personal inventory, and when we are wrong, we promptly admitted it.*

    a.   This is the new process in which I live.

        i.   Continue to look for:

            a) Selfishness

            b) Dishonesty

            c) Resentment

            d) Fear

        ii.   When found, we ask our higher power to remove them

        iii.   Discuss with someone else promptly

        iv.   Make amends if necessary

        v.   Help others: Turn your thoughts to someone you can help. This helps get me out of my crazy thinking (the real problem). One thing you can do is simply helping someone with their groceries.

11. *We seek, through prayer and meditation, to improve our conscious contact with our higher power as we understand it, praying only for knowledge of our higher power's will for us and the power to carry that out.* This is an active practice.

    a.   What does prayer and meditation look like to you?

b.   The Big Book has clear examples of how to start or ways to try on pages 84-86.

12. *Completing the circle:* Having had a spiritual awakening as a result of these steps, we try to carry this message to other addicts, and to practice these principles in all our affairs. The idea is it's my obligation to help someone else who wants my help.

a.   What's a spiritual awakening? It is different for everybody. It can even be of the educational variety: you wake up and realize you haven't lied, cheated, or stolen in years. "I have a job, I have a relationship, I have insurance." Or, "I haven't drunk today, and I haven't thought about it." Sometimes, people feel it more emotionally.

b.   What does it mean to practice these principles in all areas of life?

c.   What does it mean to be a sponsor?

d.   How else can I carry this message?

About the Author

Kevin Petersen, MA, LMFT, is the founder of The Chronic Hope Institute, which provides healing for families in crisis due to addiction and codependency, and family case management training for clinicians. In 2011, Kevin graduated with a master's degree in Marriage and Family Therapy from Regis University, and he spent three and a half years working at Arapahoe Douglas Mental Health Network as an in-home therapist, case manager, crisis evaluator and outpatient therapist for Child and Family Services. Kevin has also worked part-time for The Bridge House, ADMHN's Acute Treatment Unit, as a Mental Health Technician and Counselor. In 2014, Kevin opened his private practice, Petersen Family Counseling, which specializes in working with families and individuals struggling with addictions, codependency, and parenting. In 2019, Kevin published Chronic Hope: Parenting the Addicted Child, an eye-opening assessment of how setting boundaries, maintaining accountability, and providing full transparency are three critical ways of turning chronic hope into a reality.

Kevin established The Chronic Hope Institute in 2020 with a mission to help families in crisis through family case management and empower mental health professionals with this training to help families. Dedicated to strengthening the family system, Kevin turns helplessness into hope.

If you are struggling with an addict and need a plan, contact The Chronic Hope Institute at www.ChronicHope.us.

Kevin began his journey of recovery in May 1991 and has been sober ever since. He lives in Florida with his wife, Amy, and three Boston Terriers Bert, Blanche and Stella.

(720) 541-6289 | Kevin@ChronicHope.us

www.chronichope.us

Twitter: @TheChronicHope

Facebook: @ChronicHopeInstitute

Instagram: @TheChronicHopeInstitute

LinkedIn: www.linkedin.com/showcase/the-chronic-hope-institute/

Podcast: Apple, Google, Spotify, YouTube, or wherever you listen!

4th Step Inventory for Family Members

Resentments – who or what are we mad at?

Who am I angry at?

What did they do to harm me?

How does this affect my:

Ambition – *I want:*

Self-Esteem – *I see myself as:*

Security – *I am safe when:*

Pride – *I deserve:*

Personal – *My friends/family think:*

Sex – *The opposite sex will think:*

_____

Pocket Book – *Money, time and effort has cost me in*

_____

Where have I been:

Selfish:

_____

Dishonest:

_____

Self-seeking:

_____

Afraid:

_____

At Fault:

_____

Fear: What am I Really Afraid Of?

Describe your fear: I'm afraid of

_____

What are you afraid will happen: I'm afraid

_____

I selfishly try to protect and preserve my life by

....

I am not trusting and relying on God to care and protect me

....

Conduct Inventory
Think of someone you've been in a relationship with.

Where have I been selfish, dishonest, and inconsiderate with them?

....

How have I hurt them?

....

....

Did I create jealousy, suspicion, or bitterness?

....

....

Where was I at fault?

....

....

What should I have done instead?

....

....

P.140 what does until the behavior changes I cant
do this. If you are going to kill yourself an
continue to be at such risk I cant do this.
Please dont call from jail. only a rehab

Hi Ross. No I've done that.
I'll talk about rehab but no # for the phone —
I'll support recovery. I've provided $ for
you to call. To do your research.
think You know the places.
Answer p. ~~141~~ ~~#~~ 142

Made in the USA
Middletown, DE
28 November 2023